Individual Rights and the Police

Other books in the Issues on Trial series:

Individual Rights and the Police

Mark R. Nesbitt, Book Editor

GREENHAVEN PRESS
An imprint of Thomson Gale, a part of The Thomson Corporation

Detroit • New York • San Francisco • San Diego • New Haven, Conn.
Waterville, Maine • London • Munich

Bonnie Szumski, *Publisher*
Helen Cothran, *Managing Editor*
Scott Barbour, *Series Editor*

For more information, contact:
Greenhaven Press
27500 Drake Rd.
Farmington Hills, MI 48331-3535
Or you can visit our Internet site at http://www.gale.com

LIBRARY OF CONGRESS CATALOGING-IN-PUBLICATION DATA

Individual Rights and the Police / Mark R. Nesbitt, book editor.
    p. cm. -- (Issues on trial)
    Includes bibliographical references and index. ISBN 0-7377-2505-2 (lib. bdg. : alk. paper)
    1. Criminal procedure--United States. 2. Civil rights--United States. I. Nesbitt, Mark R., 1970–. II. Series.
    KF9618.R54 2006
    345.73'056--dc22

                                                                            2005054542

Contents

A law professor maintains that *Mapp* was a positive development for the protection of African Americans in the criminal justice system, but subsequent decisions have undermined its impact.

Chapter 2: Securing the Right Against Self-Incrimination

A constitutional scholar argues that rather than over-turning *Miranda*, the Court should modify it to allow suspects to be interrogated without their lawyers present.

Chapter 3: Defining the Right to Privacy

Chapter 4: The Power of the Police to Stop and Frisk

Foreword

The U.S. courts have long served as a battleground for the most highly charged and contentious issues of the time. Divisive matters are often brought into the legal system by activists who feel strongly for their cause and demand an official resolution. Indeed, subjects that give rise to intense emotions or involve closely held religious or moral beliefs lay at the heart of the most polemical court rulings in history. One such case was *Brown v. Board of Education* (1954), which ended racial segregation in schools. Prior to *Brown*, the courts had held that blacks could be forced to use separate facilities as long as these facilities were equal to that of whites.

For years many groups had opposed segregation based on religious, moral, and legal grounds. Educators produced heartfelt testimony that segregated schooling greatly disadvantaged black children. They noted that in comparison to whites, blacks received a substandard education in deplorable conditions. Religious leaders such as Martin Luther King Jr. preached that the harsh treatment of blacks was immoral and unjust. Many involved in civil rights law, such as Thurgood Marshall, called for equal protection of all people under the law, as their study of the Constitution had indicated that segregation was illegal and un-American. Whatever their motivation for ending the practice, and despite the threats they received from segregationists, these ardent activists remained unwavering in their cause.

Those fighting against the integration of schools were mainly white southerners who did not believe that whites and blacks should intermingle. Blacks were subordinate to whites, they maintained, and society had to resist any attempt to break down strict color lines. Some white southerners charged that segregated schooling was *not* hindering blacks' education. For example, Virginia attorney general J. Lindsay Almond asserted, "With the help and the sympathy and the love and respect of the white people of the South, the colored man has risen under that educational process to a place of eminence and respect throughout the nation. It has served him well." So when the Supreme Court ruled against the segregationists in *Brown*, the South responded with vociferous cries of protest. Even government leaders criticized the decision. The governor of Arkansas, Orval Faubus, stated that he would not "be a party to any attempt to force acceptance of change to which the people are so overwhelmingly opposed." Indeed, resistance to integration was so great that when black students arrived at the formerly all-white Central High School in Arkansas, federal troops had to be dispatched to quell a threatening mob of protesters.

Nevertheless, the *Brown* decision was enforced and the South integrated its schools. In this instance, the Court, while not settling the issue to everyone's satisfaction, functioned as an instrument of progress by forcing a major social change. Historian David Halberstam observes that the *Brown* ruling "deprived segregationist practices of their moral legitimacy. . . . It was therefore perhaps the single most important moment of the decade, the moment that separated the old order from the new and helped create the tumultuous era just arriving." Considered one of the most important victories for civil rights, *Brown* paved the way for challenges to racial segregation in many areas, including on public buses and in restaurants.

In examining *Brown*, it becomes apparent that the courts play an influential role—and face an arduous challenge—in shaping the debate over emotionally charged social issues. Judges must balance competing interests, keeping in mind the high stakes and intense emotions on both sides. As exemplified by *Brown*, judicial decisions often upset the status quo and initiate significant changes in society. Greenhaven Press's Issues on Trial series captures the controversy surrounding influential court rulings and explores the social ramifications of such decisions from varying perspectives. Each anthology highlights one social issue—such as the death penalty, students' rights, or wartime civil liberties. Each volume then focuses on key historical and contemporary court cases that helped mold the issue as we know it today. The books include a compendium of primary sources—court rulings, dissents, and immediate reactions to the rulings—as well as secondary sources from experts in the field, people involved in the cases, legal analysts, and other commentators opining on the implications and legacy of the chosen cases. An annotated table of contents, an in-depth introduction, and prefaces that overview each case all provide context as readers delve into the topic at hand. To help students fully probe the subject, each volume contains book and periodical bibliographies, a comprehensive index, and a list of organizations to contact. With these features, the Issues on Trial series offers a well-rounded perspective on the courts' role in framing society's thorniest, most impassioned debates.

Introduction

On October 13, 1995, the Miami-Dade police received an anonymous tip that a young black man in a plaid shirt was at a bus stop with a gun. Acting on the tip, the police arrived on the scene and found three young men, one of whom was wearing a plaid shirt. The officers searched him and found a gun. They placed him in custody, and he was later tried and convicted of carrying an illegal, concealed firearm.

The young man, known as J.L. in court documents, appealed the conviction. His appeal eventually made its way to the Supreme Court. In March 2000 the Court ruled that the search was illegal because a police officer can search an individual only if he or she obtains a warrant or has probable cause—that is, reasonable ground for suspicion that a crime has been committed or will soon be committed. The officers in this instance did not have a warrant and had not observed any suspicious behavior by the suspect that could constitute probable cause. J.L. was released even though he had indeed broken the law by carrying an illegal weapon.

A Check on Police Power

The J.L. case illustrates one of the greatest challenges of the criminal justice system in the United States—balancing the ability of the police to enforce the law and the rights of citizens to privacy and freedom. Police officers must obtain information and evidence about suspects while investigating or attempting to prevent crimes. The process of obtaining evidence may involve searching the suspect's person, home, or belongings; seizing the suspect's documents and possessions; observing the suspect; and listening to the suspect's conversations. Such evidence enables the police to convict the guilty or prevent a crime. However, every citizen of the United States is entitled to a number of rights that limit and regulate these evidence-gathering procedures. These rights, found mainly in the Fourth and Fifth Amendments to the Constitution, act as a check against the power of the government to monitor its citizens.

The framers of the Constitution were well aware of the dangers of a government with unchecked power to investigate people. As stated by law professor Melvyn Zarr, "They recognized the tendency of even well-meaning officials, once caught up in the excitement of pursuit of suspected criminals, to use whatever short-cut seemed most effective and to ignore the liberties of the citizenry."[1] They sought to prevent the abuses common under eighteenth-century English law, which allowed officials to search and seize the property of anyone for virtually any reason. Consequently, they wrote the Fourth and Fifth Amendments, which became part of the Bill of Rights. The Fourth Amendment protects citizens against "unreasonable searches and seizures." It also states that no search warrant shall be issued without probable cause. The Fifth Amendment, among other rights, protects suspects from being held without indictment for a crime and grants them the right not to make incriminating statements about themselves.

Upholding the Rights of Suspects

The rights of suspects have been reinforced by many Supreme Court decisions throughout the years. For instance, as early as 1886, the Court was called on to interpret the Fourth and Fifth Amendments in the case of *Boyd v. United States*. A man named Boyd had been charged with smuggling and was ordered to turn over his personal papers. A lower court had ruled that if he refused, he would be convicted of the crime. The Supreme Court reversed this decision on the grounds that requiring Boyd to turn over his papers was an illegal seizure in violation of the Fourth Amendment. In addition, the Court declared, it violated Boyd's Fifth Amendment right not to incriminate himself.

Another Supreme Court ruling that expanded the rights of suspects was the 1914 case of *Weeks v. United States.* In this ruling the Supreme Court extended the protection of the Fourth Amendment by creating the "exclusionary rule," which forbids evidence obtained during an illegal search to be used in a trial. Prior to this decision, even if a search was deemed illegal, the evidence found during the search could still be used in court. The exclusionary rule changed law enforcement because otherwise credible evidence could now be excluded from a case due to a technicality such as the wrong address on a search warrant. As legal historian Morton J. Horwitz states, "The downside of the exclusionary rule was that it also meant depriving juries of reliable evidence of the defendant's guilt."[2] The Supreme Court had again sided with the individual and placed the burden of procedure on the police in order to protect the rights of suspects.

In the 1960s the Warren Court (the Supreme Court under Chief Justice Earl Warren) heard a series of cases dealing with the Fourth and Fifth Amendments. In a majority of those cases the Court ruled in favor of the suspect rather than the police, upholding and expanding suspects' freedom from unreasonable search and seizure, the right to counsel, and the right against self-incrimination. All of these rulings—from the *Boyd* decision through the rulings of the Warren Court—firmly established the rights of the individual.

Not Absolute Rights

However, the rights guaranteed by the Fourth and Fifth Amendments are not absolute. The Supreme Court has ruled that not every search requires a warrant in order to be considered reasonable. In many circumstances a warrantless search is considered reasonable as long as there is probable cause. For example, in *Chimel v. California* (1969) the Court declared that when an arrest has taken place, the suspect and the surrounding area can be searched for evidence. In addition, a warrant is not required for a police officer to seize evidence that is in plain view, such as cocaine seen on the seat of a car during a traffic stop. Moreover, if an officer is in "hot pursuit" of a criminal, he or she may follow the suspect into a building and seize any evidence found in the process. These are just a few examples of legal warrantless searches.

In addition to exceptions to the warrant requirement, in many situations not even probable cause is required for a search to be deemed legal. In *Terry v. Ohio* (1968) the Supreme Court declared that police may stop and frisk a suspect for weapons based merely on their suspicion that the suspect might be armed. In addition, due to the threat of terrorism, airline travelers may be subjected to searches without probable cause. Students also can be subjected to various types of searches without probable cause. In *New Jersey v. T.L.O.* (1985) the Court ruled that school officials can search students without probable cause. And in *Vernonia School District 47J v. Acton* (1995) the Court declared that probable cause is not required in order to test student athletes for drug use. As these and other examples reveal, the Court has found numerous exceptions to Americans' Fourth and Fifth Amendment rights.

Balancing Individual Rights and Social Order

When dealing with the rights of those suspected of a crime, the Supreme Court of the United States must strive to decide cases according to the Constitution in such a way as to best serve both the individual as well as the good of society. It must strike a balance between protecting the rights and freedoms of an individual while still being able to find and punish the guilty. In order to appreciate and understand the challenge that faces the United States in maintaining this balance, this volume examines four cases that have helped shape the discussion: *Mapp v. Ohio* (1961), *Miranda v. Arizona* (1966), *Katz v. United States* (1967), and *Terry v. Ohio* (1968). The Court's opinions and dissentions from each ruling, as well analysis of each decision, will help in understanding the tension between the rights of individuals and the need to enforce the law.

Notes

1. Melvyn Zarr, *The Bill of Rights and the Police*. Dobbs Ferry, NY: Oceana, 1980, p. 1.
2. Morton J. Horwitz, *The Warren Court and the Pursuit of Justice: A Critical Issue*. New York: Hill and Wang, 1998, p. 97.

CHAPTER 1

| Limiting Illegal Search

Case Overview

Mapp v. Ohio (1961)

In *Mapp v. Ohio* (1961) the U.S. Supreme Court concluded that the exclusionary rule, which forbade the use of illegally obtained evidence in a federal court, must also be applied to state courts. Prior to this ruling individual state courts were allowed to decide whether or not evidence obtained illegally (that is, without a warrant) could be used at trial on a case-by-case basis. An earlier Supreme Court ruling, *Wolf v. Colorado* (1949), had supported this interpretation and allowed state courts their latitude. *Mapp* overturned *Wolf* and extended the exclusionary rule to all courts—state and federal.

The *Mapp* case arose when Cleveland police received a tip that a bombing suspect was hiding in the residence of Dollree Mapp. Police came to the Mapp residence on May 23, 1957, demanding entrance. Mapp, acting on the advice of her lawyer, refused their request because they did not have a warrant. The police later returned with a piece of paper that they claimed was a warrant. Mapp asked to see the warrant and was refused. She grabbed the paper from the police officer, who then arrested her. A subsequent search of her home found obscene materials, which was a violation of an Ohio state law.

Based on the evidence removed from her home, Mapp was convicted of possession of obscene materials. During the trial Mapp's attorney requested that the police produce the warrant. They were unable or unwilling to do so. Mapp appealed her conviction on the grounds that the search that had led to the evidence was unlawful because it had been conducted without a warrant. The Ohio Supreme Court then ruled that the conviction should stand. It claimed that while a reasonable argument could be made that the evidence should be suppressed, the Fourth Amendment protection against unlawful search had not been applied to the state courts. Mapp then appealed to the Supreme Court.

On June 19, 1961, the Court ruled 6-3 to overturn Mapp's conviction. This decision was based primarily on two amendments to the Constitution and two prior cases that dealt with them. In *Weeks v. United States* (1914) the Supreme Court had ruled that the Fourth Amendment protects an individual from warrantless searches and that evidence obtained from such searches cannot be used in federal court, thus establishing the exclusionary rule. In *Wolf v. Colorado,* the Court had stated that the Fourteenth Amendment, which provides for due process under the law for all citizens, applies the Bill of Rights, and thus the Fourth Amendment, to the states as well as the federal government. However, the Court also ruled that the exclusionary rule established in *Weeks* did not apply to the states. In *Mapp* the Court ruled that this distinction was unfounded and that the entire scope of the Fourth Amendment should be applied to state courts. Thus the exclusionary rule must be enforced at the state level.

Later rulings have modified *Mapp. Nix v. Williams* (1984) allowed evidence obtained without a warrant to be included in a trial if the discovery of the evidence was seen as inevitable given the facts of the case. Also, in *U.S. v. Leon* (1984) the Court ruled that if the police were acting on good faith with a warrant that was later ruled invalid due to a clerical error, the evidence found with that warrant could still be admissible.

"We hold that all evidence obtained by searches and seizures in violation of the Constitution is, by that same authority, inadmissible in a state court."

The Court's Decision: Illegally Obtained Evidence Cannot Be Used in Court

Thomas Campbell Clark

Thomas Campbell Clark was appointed to the U.S. Supreme Court in 1949 and served for eighteen years. He is best known for writing the majority opinions in Abington School District v. Schempp, *the case that removed daily Bible readings from public schools, and* Mapp v. Ohio.

The following selection is excerpted from Clark's opinion in Mapp v. Ohio, *a case that dealt with the issue of illegal searches. The Fourth Amendment of the U.S. Constitution forbids the government from subjecting people to "unreasonable searches" in pursuit of incriminating evidence. In* Weeks v. United States *(1914) the Supreme Court ruled that the government was not only barred from conducting such searches; it was barred from using any evidence obtained from an illegal search against a suspect in federal court. This ban on illegally obtained evidence became known as the exclusionary rule. However, the exclusionary rule did not apply to state courts; state prosecutors were free to use illegally obtained evidence in their cases against criminal suspects. In* Wolf v. Colorado *(1949) the Court declined to extend the exclusionary rule to state courts.*

In Mapp v. Ohio, *however, the Court reversed itself and ruled that any evidence obtained in an illegal search could not*

Thomas Campbell Clark, majority opinion, *Mapp v. Ohio*, June 19, 1961.

be used against a suspect in either a federal or a state court. Clark cites both the Fourth and the Fourteenth Amendments in arguing that the right against unfair searches and seizures deserves the highest level of protection.

In 1949, 35 years after *Weeks* [*v. United States* (1914)] was announced, this Court, in *Wolf v. Colorado*, . . . for the first time, discussed the effect of the Fourth Amendment upon the States through the operation of the Due Process Clause of the Fourteenth Amendment. It said:

> We have no hesitation in saying that were a State affirmatively to sanction such police incursion into privacy it would run counter to the guaranty of the Fourteenth Amendment.

Nevertheless, after declaring that the "security of one's privacy against arbitrary intrusion by the police" is "implicit in the concept of ordered liberty and as such enforceable against the States through the Due Process Clause," and announcing that it "stoutly adhered" to the *Weeks* decision, the Court decided that the *Weeks* exclusionary rule would not then be imposed upon the States as "an essential ingredient of the right." . . .

Wolf Is No Longer Valid

While in 1949, prior to the *Wolf* case, almost two-thirds of the States were opposed to the use of the exclusionary rule, now, despite the *Wolf* case, more than half of those since passing upon it, by their own legislative or judicial decision, have wholly or partly adopted or adhered to the *Weeks* rule. . . .

Likewise, time has set its face against what *Wolf* called the "weighty testimony" of *People v. Defore* (1926). There Justice (then Judge) [Benjamin] Cardozo, rejecting adoption of the *Weeks* exclusionary rule in New York, had said that "the Federal rule as it stands is either too strict or too lax." However, the force of that reasoning has been largely vitiated by later decisions of this Court. . . .

It, therefore, plainly appears that the factual considerations supporting the failure of the *Wolf* Court to include the *Weeks* exclusionary rule when it recognized the enforceability of the right to privacy against the States in 1949, while not basically relevant to the constitutional consideration, could not, in any analysis, now be deemed controlling.

Application of Exclusionary Rule to States

Some five years after *Wolf*, in answer to a plea made here Term after Term that we overturn its doctrine on applicability of the *Weeks* exclusionary rule, this Court indicated that such should not be done until the States had "adequate opportunity to adopt or reject the [*Weeks*] rule." *Irvine v. California.* There again it was said:

> Never until June of 1949 did this Court hold the basic search-and-seizure prohibition in any way applicable to the states under the Fourteenth Amendment.

And only last Term [in late 1960], after again carefully re-examining the *Wolf* doctrine in *Elkins v. United States*, the Court pointed out that "the controlling principles" as to search and seizure and the problem of admissibility "seemed clear" until the announcement in *Wolf* "that the Due Process Clause of the Fourteenth Amendment does not itself require state courts to adopt the exclusionary rule" of the *Weeks* case. . . . The Court concluded that it was therefore obliged to hold . . . that all evidence obtained by an unconstitutional search and seizure was inadmissible in a federal court regardless of its source. Today we once again examine *Wolf's* constitutional documentation of the right to privacy free from unreasonable state intrusion, and, after its dozen years on our books, are led by it to close the only courtroom door remaining open to evidence secured by official lawlessness in flagrant abuse of that basic right, reserved to all persons as a specific guarantee against that very same unlawful conduct. We hold that all evidence obtained by searches and seizures in violation of the Constitution is, by that same authority, inadmissible in a state court.

Protection of Privacy Must Be Enforced

Since the Fourth Amendment's right of privacy has been declared enforceable against the States through the Due Process Clause of the Fourteenth [Amendment], it is enforceable against them by the same sanction of exclusion as is used against the Federal Government. Were it otherwise, then just as without the *Weeks* rule the assurance against unreasonable federal searches and seizures would be "a form of words," valueless and undeserving of mention in a perpetual charter of inestimable human liberties, so too, without that rule the freedom from state invasions of privacy would be so ephemeral and so neatly severed from its conceptual nexus with the freedom from all brutish means of coercing evidence as not to merit this Court's high regard as a freedom "implicit in the concept of ordered liberty." At the time that the Court held in *Wolf* that the Amendment was applicable to the States through the Due Process Clause, the cases of this Court . . . had steadfastly held that as to federal officers the Fourth Amendment included the exclusion of the evidence seized in violation of its provisions. Even *Wolf* "stoutly adhered" to that proposition. . . . In extending the substantive protections of due process to all constitutionally unreasonable searches—state or federal—it was logically and constitutionally necessary that the exclusion doctrine—an essential part of the right to privacy—be also insisted upon as an essential ingredient of the right newly recognized by the *Wolf* case. In short, the admission of the new constitutional right by *Wolf* could not consistently tolerate denial of its most important constitutional privilege, namely, the exclusion of the evidence which an accused had been forced to give by reason of the unlawful seizure. To hold otherwise is to grant the right but in reality to withhold its privilege and enjoyment. . . .

Indeed, we are aware of no restraint, similar to that rejected today, conditioning the enforcement of any other basic constitutional right. The right to privacy, no less important than any other right carefully and particularly reserved to the people, would stand in marked contrast to all other rights declared as "basic to a free society." *Wolf v. Colorado*. This Court has not hesitated to enforce as strictly against the States as it does against the Federal Government the rights of free speech and of a free press, the rights to notice and to a fair, public trial, including, as it does, the right not to be convicted by use of a coerced confession, however logically relevant it be, and without regard to its reliability. And nothing could be more certain than that when a coerced confession is involved, "the relevant rules of evidence" are overridden without regard to "the incidence of such conduct by the police," slight or frequent. Why should not the same rule apply to what is tantamount to coerced testimony by way of unconstitutional seizure of goods, papers, effects, documents, etc.? We find that, as to the Federal Government, the Fourth and Fifth Amendments and, as to the States, the freedom from unconscionable invasions of privacy and the freedom from convictions based upon coerced confessions do enjoy an "intimate relation" in their perpetuation of "principles of humanity and civil liberty [secured] . . . only after years of struggle," *Bram v. United States* (1897). They express "supplementing phases of the same constitutional purpose—to maintain inviolate large areas of personal privacy." *Feldman v. United States* (1944). The philosophy of each Amendment and of each freedom is complementary to, although not dependent upon, that of the other in its sphere of influence—the very least that together they assure in either sphere is that no man is to be convicted on unconstitutional evidence.

Law and Reason

Moreover, our holding that the exclusionary rule is an essential part of both the Fourth and Fourteenth Amendments is not only the logical dictate of prior cases, but it also makes very good sense. There is no war between the Constitution and common sense. Presently, a federal prosecutor may make no use of evidence illegally seized, but a State's attorney across the street may, although he supposedly is operating under the enforceable prohibitions of the same Amendment. Thus the State, by admitting evidence unlawfully seized, serves to encourage disobedience to the Federal Constitution which it is bound to uphold. Moreover, as was said in *Elkins*, "the very essence of a healthy federalism depends upon the avoidance of needless conflict between state and federal courts." Yet the double standard recognized until today hardly put such a thesis into practice. In nonexclusionary States, federal officers, being human, were by it invited to and did . . . step across the street to the State's attorney with their unconstitutionally seized evidence. Prosecution on the basis of that evidence was then had in a state court in utter disregard of the enforceable Fourth Amendment. If the fruits of an unconstitutional search had been inadmissible in both state and federal courts, this inducement to evasion would have been sooner eliminated. . . .

Federal-state cooperation in the solution of crime under constitutional standards will be promoted, if only by recognition of their now mutual obligation to respect the same fundamental criteria in their approaches. . . .

No Harm to Law Enforcement

There are those who say, as did Justice (then Judge) Cardozo, that under our constitutional exclusionary doctrine "the criminal is to go free because the constable has blundered." *People v. Defore*. In some cases this will undoubtedly be the result. But, as was said in *Elkins*, "there is another consideration—the imperative of judicial integrity." The criminal goes free, if he must, but it is the law that sets him free. Nothing can destroy a government more quickly than its failure to observe its own laws, or worse, its disregard of the charter of its own existence. As Mr. Justice [Louis] Brandeis, dissenting, said in *Olm-*

stead v. United States (1928): "Our Government is the potent, the omnipresent teacher. For good or for ill, it teaches the whole people by its example. . . . If the Government becomes a lawbreaker, it breeds contempt for law; it invites every man to become a law unto himself; it invites anarchy." Nor can it lightly be assumed that, as a practical matter, adoption of the exclusionary rule fetters law enforcement. Only last year [in 1960] this Court expressly considered that contention and found that "pragmatic evidence of a sort" to the contrary was not wanting. *Elkins v. United States.*

The ignoble shortcut to conviction left open to the State tends to destroy the entire system of constitutional restraints on which the liberties of the people rest. Having once recognized that the right to privacy embodied in the Fourth Amendment is enforceable against the States, and that the right to be secure against rude invasions of privacy by state officers is, therefore, constitutional in origin, we can no longer permit that right to remain an empty promise. Because it is enforceable in the same manner and to like effect as other basic rights secured by the Due Process Clause, we can no longer permit it to be revocable at the whim of any police officer who, in the name of law enforcement itself, chooses to suspend its enjoyment. Our decision, founded on reason and truth, gives to the individual no more than that which the Constitution guarantees him, to the police officer no less than that to which honest law enforcement is entitled, and, to the courts, that judicial integrity so necessary in the true administration of justice.

"I would not impose upon the States this federal exclusionary remedy."

Dissenting Opinion: Illegally Obtained Evidence Should Not Be Excluded from State Trials

John Marshall Harlan II

John Marshall Harlan II, the grandson of a Supreme Court justice, served on the Court from 1955 until his death on December 30, 1971. Harlan was known for siding with precedent, which led to the dissent he wrote in the case of Mapp v. Ohio. *In* Mapp, *the Court extended the exclusionary rule, which bars the use of illegally obtained evidence in a trial, to state courts as well as federal courts. In the process it overturned a previous Court decision,* Wolf v. Colorado.

In his opinion Harlan argues that Wolf *should not be overruled. He contends that the Court's ruling is wrong in deciding that the exclusionary rule is a fundamental right that applies to the states under the Fourteenth Amendment. Instead, he insists that the states should be free to establish their own judicial procedures and choose for themselves whether to adopt the exclusionary rule.*

In overruling the *Wolf [v. Colorado]* case [1949] the Court, in my opinion, has forgotten the sense of judicial restraint which, with due regard for stare decisis,[1] is one element that

---

1. the theory that past legal decisions should stand unless they are found to violate basic principles of justice

John Marshall Harlan II, dissenting opinion, *Mapp v. Ohio*, June 19, 1961.

should enter into deciding whether a past decision of this Court should be overruled. Apart from that I also believe that the *Wolf* rule represents sounder Constitutional doctrine than the new rule which now replaces it.

From the Court's statement of the case one would gather that the central, if not controlling, issue on this appeal is whether illegally state-seized evidence is Constitutionally admissible in a state prosecution, an issue which would of course face us with the need for re-examining *Wolf*. However, such is not the situation. For, although that question was indeed raised here and below among appellant's subordinate points, the new and pivotal issue brought to the Court by this appeal is whether 2905.34 of the Ohio Revised Code making criminal the mere knowing possession or control of obscene material, and under which appellant has been convicted, is consistent with the rights of free thought and expression assured against state action by the Fourteenth Amendment. That was the principal issue which was decided by the Ohio Supreme Court, which was tendered by appellant's Jurisdictional Statement, and which was briefed and argued in this Court.

In this posture of things, I think it fair to say that five members of this Court have simply "reached out" to overrule *Wolf*. With all respect for the views of the majority, and recognizing that stare decisis carries different weight in Constitutional adjudication than it does in nonconstitutional decision, I can perceive no justification for regarding this case as an appropriate occasion for re-examining *Wolf*....

Having been unable, however, to persuade any of the majority to a different procedural course, I now turn to the merits of the present decision.

A Mistaken Argument

Essential to the majority's argument against *Wolf* is the proposition that the rule of *Weeks v. United States* [1914], excluding in federal criminal trials the use of evidence obtained in violation of the Fourth Amendment, derives not from the "supervisory power" of this Court over the federal judicial system, but from Constitutional requirement. This is so because no one, I suppose, would suggest that this Court possesses any general supervisory power over the state courts. Although I entertain considerable doubt as to the soundness of this foundational proposition of the majority, I shall assume, for present purposes, that the *Weeks* rule "is of constitutional origin."

At the heart of the majority's opinion in this case is the following syllogism: (1) the rule excluding in federal criminal trials evidence which is the product of an illegal search and seizure is "part and parcel" of the Fourth Amendment; (2) *Wolf* held that the "privacy" assured against federal action by the Fourth Amendment is also protected against state action by the Fourteenth Amendment; and (3) it is therefore "logically and constitutionally necessary" that the *Weeks* exclusionary rule should also be enforced against the States.

This reasoning ultimately rests on the unsound premise that because *Wolf* carried into the States, as part of "the concept of ordered liberty" embodied in the Fourteenth Amendment, the principle of "privacy" underlying the Fourth Amendment, it must follow that whatever configurations of the Fourth Amendment have been developed in the particularizing federal precedents are likewise to be deemed a part of "ordered liberty," and as such are enforceable against the States. For me, this does not follow at all.

Imposing a Federal Remedy on the States

It cannot be too much emphasized that what was recognized in *Wolf* was not that the Fourth Amendment as such is enforceable against the States as a facet of due process, a view of the Fourteenth Amendment which, as *Wolf* itself pointed out, has long since been discredited, but the principle of privacy "which is at the core of the Fourth Amendment." It would not be proper to expect or impose any precise equivalence, either as regards the scope of the right or the means of its implementation, between the requirements of the Fourth and Fourteenth Amendments. For the Fourth, unlike what was said in *Wolf* of the Fourteenth, does not state a general principle only; it is a particular command, having its setting in a pre-existing legal context on which both interpreting decisions and enabling statutes must at least build.

Thus, even in a case which presented simply the question of whether a particular search and seizure was constitutionally "unreasonable"—say in a tort action against state officers—we would not be true to the Fourteenth Amendment were we merely to stretch the general principle of individual privacy on a Procrustean bed of federal precedents under the Fourth Amendment. But in this instance more than that is involved, for here we are reviewing not a determination that what the state police did was Constitutionally permissible (since the state court quite evidently assumed that it was not), but a determination that appellant was properly found guilty of conduct which, for present purposes, it is to be assumed the State could Constitutionally punish. Since there is not the slightest suggestion that Ohio's policy is "affirmatively to sanction . . . police incursion into privacy" . . . [*Marcus v. Search Warrants*], what the Court is now doing is to impose upon the States not only federal substantive standards of "search and seizure" but also the basic federal remedy for violation of those standards. For I think it entirely clear that the *Weeks* exclusionary rule is but a remedy which, by penalizing past official misconduct, is aimed at deterring such conduct in the future.

I would not impose upon the States this federal exclusionary remedy. The reasons given by the majority for now suddenly turning its back on *Wolf* seem to me notably unconvincing.

Voluntary State Action Should Be Preserved

First, it is said that "the factual grounds upon which *Wolf* was based" have since changed, in that more States now follow the *Weeks* exclusionary rule than was so at the time *Wolf* was decided. While that is true, a recent survey indicates that at present one-half of the States still adhere to the common-law non-exclusionary rule, and one, Maryland, retains the rule as to felonies. But in any case surely all this is beside the point, as the majority itself indeed seems to recognize. Our concern here, as it was in *Wolf*, is not with the desirability of that rule but only with the question whether the States are Constitutionally free to follow it or not as they may themselves determine, and the relevance of the disparity of views among the States on this point lies simply in the fact that the judgment involved is a debatable one. Moreover, the very fact on which the majority relies, instead of lending support to what is now being done, points away from the need of replacing voluntary state action with federal compulsion.

The preservation of a proper balance between state and federal responsibility in the administration of criminal justice demands patience on the part of those who might like to see things move faster among the States in this respect. Problems of criminal law enforcement vary widely from State to State. . . . In my view this Court should continue to forbear from fettering the States with an adamant rule which may embarrass them in coping with their own peculiar problems in criminal law enforcement.

States Should Be Allowed to Establish Procedures

Further, we are told that imposition of the *Weeks* rule on the States makes "very good sense," in that it will promote recognition by state and federal officials of their "mutual obligation to respect the same fundamental criteria" in their approach to law enforcement, and will avoid "needless conflict between state and federal courts." Indeed the majority now finds an in-congruity in *Wolf*'s discriminating perception between the de-mands of "ordered liberty" as respects the basic right of "pri-vacy" and the means of securing it among the States. That perception, resting both on a sensitive regard for our federal system and a sound recognition of this Court's remoteness from particular state problems, is for me the strength of that decision.

An approach which regards the issue as one of achieving procedural symmetry or of serving administrative convenience surely disfigures the boundaries of this Court's functions in relation to the state and federal courts. Our role in promul-gating the *Weeks* rule and its extensions in . . . other cases was quite a different one than it is here. There, in implementing the Fourth Amendment, we occupied the position of a tribu-nal having the ultimate responsibility for developing the stan-dards and procedures of judicial administration within the ju-dicial system over which it presides. Here we review state procedures whose measure is to be taken not against the spe-cific substantive commands of the Fourth Amendment but under the flexible contours of the Due Process Clause. I do not believe that the Fourteenth Amendment empowers this Court to mould state remedies effectuating the right to free-dom from "arbitrary intrusion by the police" to suit its own notions of how things should be done. . . .

A False Analogy

Finally, it is said that the overruling of *Wolf* is supported by the established doctrine that the admission in evidence of an involuntary confession renders a state conviction Constitu-tionally invalid. Since such a confession may often be entirely reliable, and therefore of the greatest relevance to the issue of the trial, the argument continues, this doctrine is ample war-rant in precedent that the way evidence was obtained, and not just its relevance, is Constitutionally significant to the fairness of a trial. I believe this analogy is not a true one. The "coerced confession" rule is certainly not a rule that any illegally obtained statements may not be used in evidence. I would suppose that a statement which is procured during a period of illegal detention, *McNabb v. United States*, is, as much as unlawfully seized evidence, illegally obtained, but this Court has consistently refused to reverse state convictions resting on the use of such statements. . . .

The point, then, must be that in requiring exclusion of an involuntary statement of an accused, we are concerned not with an appropriate remedy for what the police have done, but with something which is regarded as going to the heart of our concepts of fairness in judicial procedure. . . . The pressures brought to bear against an accused leading to a confession, unlike an unconstitutional violation of privacy, do not, apart from the use of the confession at trial, necessarily involve independent Constitutional violations. What is crucial is that the trial defense to which an accused is entitled should not be rendered an empty formality by reason of statements wrung from him. . . . That this is a procedural right, and that its violation occurs at the time his improperly obtained statement is admitted at trial, is manifest. For without this right all the careful safeguards erected around the giving of testimony, whether by an accused or any other witness, would become empty formalities in a procedure where the most compelling possible evidence of guilt, a confession, would have already been obtained at the unsupervised pleasure of the police.

This, and not the disciplining of the police, as with illegally seized evidence, is surely the true basis for excluding a statement of the accused which was unconstitutionally obtained. In sum, I think the coerced confession analogy works strongly against what the Court does today. . . .

I regret that I find so unwise in principle and so inexpedient in policy a decision motivated by the high purpose of increasing respect for Constitutional rights. But in the last analysis I think this Court can increase respect for the Constitution only if it rigidly respects the limitations which the Constitution places upon it, and respects as well the principles inherent in its own processes. In the present case I think we exceed both, and that our voice becomes only a voice of power, not of reason.

> *"Police practices and prosecution proce-*
> *dures were revolutionized in many*
> *states by the holding in . . .* Mapp v.
> Ohio.*"*

The *Mapp* Ruling Was Necessary to Protect Suspects' Rights

Yale Kamisar

Yale Kamisar is a professor of law at the University of Michigan Law School. He is an expert on constitutional and criminal law who has written many articles and books, including Police Interrogation and Confessions: Essays in Law and Policy. *He is also coauthor of* Criminal Justice in Our Time *and* The Supreme Court: Trends and Developments.

In the article that follows, Kamisar defends the Court's ruling in Mapp v. Ohio, *which extended the application of the exclusionary rule to state courts. Prior to* Mapp *the exclusionary rule, which holds that evidence seized during an unlawful search cannot be used against a suspect, had applied only to federal courts. The exclusionary rule has long been under attack by those who see it as unfairly benefiting criminals. Law enforcement agencies have argued that the rule, while seeking to protect the average citizen against unlawful invasion, has instead allowed many guilty parties to go free. They contend that there are less cumbersome, alternate means for protecting people's right to be free of unfair searches and seizures. Kamisar rejects this contention, citing evidence of gross violations of suspects' Fourth Amendment rights in the absence of the exclusionary rule.*

Yale Kamisar, "In Defense of the Search and Seizure Exclusionary Rule," *Harvard Journal of Law & Public Policy*, vol. 29, Winter 2003, pp. 122–29, 131–34. Copyright © 2003 by *Harvard Journal of Law & Public Policy*. Reproduced by permission.

Perhaps we should begin with *People v. Cahan*, the pre-*Mapp* [*v. Ohio*] case in which California adopted the exclusionary rule on its own initiative. At first, Justice Roger Traynor, who wrote the majority opinion, had not been a proponent of the exclusionary rule. Indeed, thirteen years earlier, he had written the opinion of the California Supreme Court reaffirming the admissibility of illegally seized evidence. By 1955, he and a majority of his colleagues felt compelled to overrule state precedents and adopt the exclusionary rule. Why? The *Cahan* majority explained:

> Other remedies have completely failed to secure compliance with the constitutional provisions on the part of police officers with the attendant result that the courts under the old rule [of admissibility] have been constantly required to participate in, and in effect condone, the lawless activities of law enforcement officers.

Justice Traynor and his colleagues seemed astounded by how casually and routinely illegally seized evidence was being offered and admitted in the California courts. After noting that Los Angeles police had candidly admitted that they had illegally installed listening devices in the defendants' homes and had described, with equal candor, how they had forcibly entered buildings without bothering to obtain warrants by breaking windows and kicking in doors. Justice Traynor observed:

> Without fear of criminal punishment or other discipline, law enforcement officers ... frankly admit their deliberate, flagrant [unconstitutional] acts. ... It is clearly apparent from their testimony that [Los Angeles police officers] casually regard [their illegal acts] as nothing more than the performance of their ordinary duties for which the City employs and pays them.

Worthless Alternatives

Perhaps we should go back in time still further, three-quarters of a century to *People v. Defore*, the occasion for Judge (later

Justice) [Benjamin] Cardozo's famous opinion explaining why New York would not adopt the federal exclusionary rule. Cardozo maintained, as have most critics of the exclusionary rule ever since, that excluding the illegally seized evidence was not the only effective way to enforce the Fourth Amendment (or its state constitutional counterpart): "The [offending] officer might have been resisted, or sued for damages, or even prosecuted for oppression. He was subject to removal or other discipline at the hands of his superiors."

Two decades later, in *Wolf v. Colorado*, when the Supreme Court declined to impose the federal exclusionary rule on the states as a matter of Fourteenth Amendment Due Process, the *Wolf* majority, per Justice [Felix] Frankfurter, made a similar argument. Indeed, the Court relied partly on what it called Cardozo's "weighty testimony" about the availability of various alternatives to the exclusionary rule.

The states that had rejected the federal exclusionary rule, Justice Frankfurter assured us, had "not left the right to privacy without other means of protection." It could not, therefore, be "regarded as a departure from basic standards to remand [victims of unlawful searches and seizures] to the remedies of private action and such protection as the internal discipline of the police, under the eyes of an alert public opinion, may afford."

A majority of the Court took a very different view of the various alternatives (perhaps one should say, theoretical alternatives) to the exclusionary rule a dozen years later when it handed down *Mapp v. Ohio*, overruling *Wolf*. This time the Court dismissed alternatives to the exclusionary rule, noting that "the experience of California that such other remedies have been worthless and futile is buttressed by the experience of other States." But the Court had nothing specific to say about the experience in any state other than California nor did it rely on empirical studies. Instead, the Court relied on comments by Justice Traynor in *Cahan*.

Asserting that the various alternatives to the exclusionary rule are worthless (or quoting statements by the California Supreme Court to the same effect) does not necessarily make them so—just as asserting (or assuming) that alternative remedies are meaningful (as both Cardozo and Frankfurter did) does not make that so. Fortunately, impressive evidence of the ineffectiveness of the so-called alternatives to the exclusionary rule does exist. But it is not to be found in the *Mapp* opinion itself. It is to be found rather in *the reaction* of law enforcement officials to the *Mapp* decision. To borrow a phrase, this reaction is the "weighty testimony" that (despite the claims of Cardozo, Frankfurter, and others) reliance on tort remedies, criminal prosecutions, and the internal discipline of the police indeed left "the right to privacy without other means of protection."

Police Reaction Proves the Need for *Mapp*

Although Michael Murphy, the police commissioner of New York City at the time, did not say so in so many words, he left no doubt that because New York courts (relying on the *Defore* case) had permitted the prosecution to use illegally seized evidence up to the time of *Mapp*, neither the commissioner nor the thousands of officers who worked for him had been taking the law of search and seizure at all seriously. As the commissioner recalled some time later:

> I can think of no decision in recent times in the field of law enforcement which had such a dramatic and traumatic effect as [*Mapp*]. As the then commissioner of the largest police force in this country I was immediately caught up in the entire problem of reevaluating our procedures, which had followed the *Defore* rule, and ... creating new policies and new instructions for the implementation of *Mapp*.... [Decisions such as *Mapp*] *create tidal waves and earthquakes* which require rebuilding of our institutions sometimes from their very foundations upward. Retraining sessions had to be held from the very top administrators down to each of

the thousands of foot patrolmen and detectives engaged in the daily basic enforcement function.

Why was *Mapp*'s effect so "dramatic and traumatic"? Why did it create "tidal waves and earthquakes"? Why did it require "retraining" from top to bottom? Had there been *any* search and seizure training before *Mapp*?

What did the commissioner mean when he told us that prior to *Mapp* his police department's procedures "had followed the *Defore* case"? *Defore* did not set forth any procedures or permit the police to establish any procedures other than those that complied with the Fourth Amendment. It did allow New York prosecutors to use illegally seized evidence, but it did not (as the commissioner seemed to think) allow New York police to commit illegal searches and seizures. Is there any better evidence of the inadequacies of the existing alternatives to the exclusionary rule than the police reaction to the imposition of the rule?

It appears that, prior to *Mapp*, New York prosecutors were also unfamiliar with and uninterested in the law of search and seizure. Professor Richard Uviller, a New York prosecuting attorney at the time *Mapp* was handed down, recalled that he "cranked out a crude summary" of federal search and seizure law just in time for the next state convention of district attorneys and that summary turned out to be "an instant runaway best seller. It was as though we had made a belated discovery that the fourth amendment applied in the State of New York. . . ." That, I think, says it all.

Examples of California and Pennsylvania

The response of New York law enforcement officials to the imposition of the search and seizure rule is hardly unique. Six years earlier, when the California Supreme Court adopted the exclusionary rule on its own initiative in *People v. Cahan*, the reaction of the Los Angeles Chief of Police, William Parker, had been quite similar to the one his New York City counterpart displayed when *Mapp* was decided.

In Pennsylvania—another state whose courts had admitted illegally seized evidence prior to *Mapp*—a young Philadelphia assistant district attorney (and a future U.S. Senator), Arlen Specter, left little doubt that in this state, too, the so-called alternative remedies to the exclusionary rule had had virtually no effect, Commissioner Murphy had likened *Mapp* to a "tidal wave" and an "earthquake"; Mr. Specter compared it to a revolution:

> Police practices and prosecution procedures were revolutionized in many states by the holding in . . . *Mapp v. Ohio* that evidence obtained from an illegal search and seizure cannot be used in a criminal proceeding. . . . [There are indications] that the imposition of the exclusionary rule upon the states is the most significant event in criminal law since the adoption of the fourteenth amendment. . . . *Mapp* has rewritten the criminal law treatise for states which had admitted evidence regardless of how it was obtained.

Mr. Specter, like Commissioner Murphy, seemed to equate the relevance of the law of search and seizure with the presence or absence of the exclusionary rule, a remedy for the violation of a body of law the police were supposed to be obeying all along:

> The *Mapp* decision has significantly impaired the ability of the police to secure evidence to convict the guilty. . . . The law abiding citizen who must walk on some Philadelphia streets at two o'clock in the morning would doubtless prefer to be subjected to a search, without any cause, and have the police do the same to the man standing idly at a corner; but that cannot be done under *Mapp*.

The Exclusionary Rule Does Not Hinder Fourth Amendment Protection

One can hear the critics of the exclusionary rule now. *Mapp v. Ohio*, some say, removed both the incentive and the opportunity to develop effective alternative means of enforcing the Fourth Amendment. Indeed, Chief Justice Warren Burger once said that "the continued existence of [the exclusionary rule] inhibits the development of rational alternatives." However, it is hard to take this argument seriously.

First of all, as opponents of the exclusionary rule never tire of telling us, large portions of police activity relating to the seizing of criminal property do not produce (and may not even have been designed to produce) incriminating evidence, and thus do not result in criminal prosecutions. Whatever the reason for the failure to impose direct sanctions on the offending officers in these instances, it cannot be the existence of the exclusionary rule. The issue need not, and should not, be framed in terms of whether we should enforce the Fourth Amendment by an exclusionary rule *or* tort remedies against the offending officers *or* departmental sanctions. [As stated by A. Kenneth Pyle] nothing prevents the use of "internal sanctions" against the police "simultaneously with the use of the exclusionary rule." After all, "no proponent of the exclusionary rule has suggested that it should act in isolation."

Moreover, blaming the failure to develop any effective "direct sanctions" against offending police officers on the exclusionary rule itself, to borrow a phrase from [Harvard law professor] Carol Steiker, "ignores history." For many decades a large number of states had no exclusionary rule, yet none of them produced any meaningful alternatives to the rule. Almost half a century passed between the time the federal courts adopted the exclusionary rule and the time the Court finally imposed the rule on the states. But in all that time, not one of the twenty-four states that still admitted illegally seized evidence on the eve of *Mapp* had developed an effective alternative to the rule. Thus, five decades of post-*Weeks* "freedom" from the inhibiting effect of the federal exclusionary rule failed to produce any meaningful alternative to the exclusionary rule in any jurisdiction.

One can hear the critics of the exclusionary rule again. Some of them are telling us that times have changed. Have they?

Legislative Reforms Are Easily Defeated

Is there any reason to believe that today's or tomorrow's politicians are, or will be, any less fearful of appearing "soft on crime" or any more interested in protecting people under investigation by the police than the politicians of any other era? Is there any reason to think that the lawmakers of our day are any more willing than their predecessors to invigorate tort remedies (or any other "direct sanction") against police officers who act overzealously in the pursuit of "criminals"?

"If anything," observes Carol Steiker, "the escalating public hysteria over violent crime from the 1960s through the present makes it is [sic] even more 'politically suicidal' today to support restrictions on police behavior than it was before 1961."
. . .

A new book by [Pitt law professor] Welsh White relates an incident that illustrates the formidable political power possessed by the law enforcement community. As the result of a lawsuit brought by an alleged victim of abusive police interrogation practices, a police investigator looked into charges against a Chicago police commander and those working for him. He concluded that for a period of more than ten years the commander and his men had been torturing suspects into confessing. In 1993, the commander was dismissed from the police force. But allegations of police misconduct continued to fill the air. For example, ten Illinois prisoners on death row maintained that the Chicago commander and his men had extracted confessions from them by torture.

In the wake of the controversy surrounding these alleged police torture cases, the Illinois legislature at one point seemed prepared to enact a law requiring the police to video or audiotape their interrogation practices. But the law enforcement community expressed its strong opposition to the bill, claiming that it would create new obstacles and expand the rights of the accused "at the expense of crime victims, public safety and law enforcement" [according to White]. The bill died in committee.

As Justice Traynor noted long ago in *Cahan*, "even when it becomes generally known that the police conduct illegal searches and seizures, public opinion is not aroused as it is in the case of other violations of constitutional rights" because illegal arrests and unlawful searches "lack the obvious brutality of coerced confessions and the third degree and do not so clearly strike at the very basis of our civil liberties as do unfair trials. . . ." Moreover, unlike the Chicago torture cases, illegal searches and seizures do not raise doubts as to a defendant's innocence. If the police and their allies can crush legislative reform efforts in the confessions area as decisively as they did in the wake of the Chicago police scandal—despite serious questions about the guilt of a number of people on death row—how much difficulty will they have defeating legislative proposals to impose direct sanctions on them for committing Fourth Amendment violations? . . .

Compromising the Exclusionary Rule

As many other critics of the exclusionary rule have done, Judge Calabresi assumes that the criminal defendant who benefits from the application of the search and seizure exclusionary rule will often be a murderer or rapist. However, an empirical study by [University of Tennessee law professor] Thomas Davies, called [by Wayne R. La Fave] "the most careful and balanced assessment conducted to date of all available empirical data," reveals that the exclusion of evidence in murder, rape, and other violent cases is exceedingly rare. "The most striking feature of the data," reports Davies, "is the concentration of illegal searches in drug arrests (and possibly weapons possession arrests) and the extremely small effects in arrests for other offenses, including violent crimes."

It may be that search and seizure problems arise much less frequently in murder, forcible rape, and other violent crime cases than they do in drug and weapons possession cases. [University of Minnesota law professor] Myron Orfield furnishes two other explanations, one encouraging, the other not.

The first explanation is that the more serious the crime, the greater the officer's desire to see the perpetrator convicted and, because the police care more about convictions in these cases, the more potent the exclusionary rule's deterrent effects. Moreover, "big cases" are more likely to involve officers in specialized units "who are more likely to take the time and care necessary to comply with the Fourth Amendment."

The second explanation is that in "heater" cases (i.e., big cases that have "the potential to arouse public ire" if the defendant "goes free" because the police violated the Fourth Amendment), many judges will feel tremendous pressure to admit the illegally seized evidence and will often find a way to do so. It is almost as if many judges, at least those who have to run for re-election, have informally adopted one law professor's proposal to make an exception to the exclusionary rule in prosecutions for treason, espionage, murder, armed robbery, and kidnapping. I find this an unfortunate and dispiriting development, but it is only one of a number of ways in which the courts have accommodated the needs of law enforcement in the exclusionary rule era.

The Warren Court has been disbanded for more than thirty years. Since then, with only a few exceptions, the Burger and Rehnquist Courts have waged a kind of "guerilla warfare" against the law of search and seizure [in the words of Albert W. Alschuler]. As a result, Judge Cardozo's oft-quoted criticism of the exclusionary rule—"the criminal is to go free because the constable has blundered"—is out of date. The Court has taken a grudging view of what amounts to a "search" or "seizure" within the meaning of the Fourth Amendment and has taken a relaxed view of what constitutes consent to an otherwise illegal search or seizure: it has so softened the "probable cause" requirement, so increased the occasions on which the police may act on the basis of "reasonable suspicion" or in the absence of any reasonable suspicion, and so narrowed the thrust of the exclusionary rule that nowadays the criminal only "goes free" if and when the constable has blundered *badly*.

Any Remedy Will Erode Rights

Judge Calabresi argues that the downsizing of the Fourth Amendment and the protections to privacy it provides, because of the pressure the exclusionary rule puts on courts to avoid freeing a guilty defendant, should make liberals hate the exclusionary rule. I think not.

A meaningful tort remedy or administrative sanction or *any other effective alternative* to the exclusionary rule would also exert strong pressure on courts to make the rules governing search and seizure more "police-friendly." As [law professor] Monrad Paulsen noted on the eve of the *Mapp* case: "Whenever the rules are enforced by meaningful sanctions, our attention is drawn to their content. The comfort of Freedom's words spoken in the abstract is always disturbed by their application to a contested instance. Any rule of police regulation enforced in fact will generate pressures to weaken the rule."

There is no denying that one of the effects of the exclusionary rule has been to diminish the protection provided by the Fourth Amendment. But this is probably the price we would have had to pay for *any* means of enforcing the Amendment that had a bite—one that actually worked.

The only time the Amendment would not impose the societal costs that critics of the exclusionary rule complain about—and the only time it would not put pressure on the courts to water down the rules governing search and seizure—would be if it were [in the words of Supreme Court justice John Paul Stevens] "an unenforced honor code that the police may follow in their discretion."

> *"The exclusionary rule has come to be accepted as a cornerstone of our jurisprudence. That violent criminals go free as a result is now accepted as the price we pay for liberty."*

Mapp Has Allowed Many Guilty People to Go Free

Leon Scully

Leon Scully is a retired lawyer. His inquiry into the history of the Mapp v. Ohio *case led him to write* Bombers, Bolsheviks, and Bootleggers: A Study in Constitutional Subversion.

In the following selection Scully describes the background and outcome of the Mapp v. Ohio *case and offers his argument for why it was misguided. The* Mapp v. Ohio *case involved the exclusionary rule, which bans the use of illegally obtained evidence in a trial. In* Mapp, *the exclusionary rule, which had previously applied only to federal courts, was extended to also apply in state courts.*

According to Scully, the Mapp *decision was a travesty because the search that originally led to Dollree Mapp's conviction on obscenity charges was legal. A search warrant had been issued, and the obscene material had been discovered in the process of a legitimate search for evidence. The defense attorneys in the case misrepresented the facts to the Supreme Court, and the prosecutor failed to correct their errors. Scully concludes that the extension of the exclusionary rule has impeded the ability of police and prosecutors to catch and convict violent criminals.*

Leon Scully, "Civil Wrongs," *National Review*, May 25, 1992, p. 22. Copyright © 1992 by National Review, Inc., 215 Lexington Ave., New York, NY 10016. Reproduced by permission.

T he exclusionary rule—which bars the use of evidence said to have been illegally obtained—was established in 1914 in *Weeks v. United States* but did little harm until it was applied to the states. So long as the *Weeks* rule was confined to federal cases, as Justice [William] Rehnquist pointed out, its chief "beneficiaries ... were smugglers, federal income tax evaders, counterfeiters, and the like." State crime is a profoundly different matter. Ninety-five per cent of the crime committed in the United States, and virtually all violent crime, comes under the jurisdiction of the states. Once the *Weeks* rule was brought to bear against the states the result was uncounted thousands of robbers, rapists, and murderers set free.

The case which accomplished this was *Mapp v. Ohio*, decided in 1961. Since then, the exclusionary rule has come to be accepted as a cornerstone of our jurisprudence. That violent criminals go free as a result is now accepted as the price we pay for liberty. But let us turn over this cornerstone and see what lies underneath. . . .

The Real Case

The real case of *Mapp v. Ohio* began with a bang at 3:45 A.M. on May 20, 1957. The bang was caused by a bomb planted under the residence of one of Cleveland's leading "policy bankers," Donald (The Kid) King.[1] The front-page headline of the *Cleveland Press* reads: "Birns Is Jailed in Bombing; Charge $1,000-a-Week Plot." Also on the front page are photos of a youthful and short-haired Donald King and of Shondor Birns, and the statement that the bomb blast "opened what police believe is a new offensive by Shondor Birns to control Cleveland's numbers racket." The bomb didn't kill the man who, with his famous "electric hair," would go on to become the world's most successful boxing promoter, but it did give

---

1. A "policy banker" is someone who runs a clearing house, where bets in the numbers racket are sorted and the winners paid. The records of bets are called "policy slips."

him quite a fright. Instead of tending to the matter himself, in the tradition of the numbers racket, he did what a good citizen should—he went to the police. The *Cleveland Plain Dealer* reported the next day that "King made history when he openly turned to police with information he said would help send someone to jail." "Shondor was one of the five pistols who bombed me," he said to reporters. One of the others he named was Virgil Ogletree, a clearinghouse operator, who was thought to be doing his clearing in the house, and in the company, of one Dollree Mapp.

It was Ogletree for whom Sergeant Carl J. Delau and patrolmen Thomas J. Dever and Michael J. Haney were looking when they arrived at 14705 Milverton Road, Miss Mapp's residence. Perhaps they had been told by King that that was where Ogletree was, so also would be a large amount of "policy paraphernalia." There is no mention of policy paraphernalia in the "official version" of the case. We are told only that the police were "ostensibly looking for an individual who was wanted in connection with an extortion bombing." And from its opinion we know the Supreme Court believed that but for the obscene material, the police came up empty handed.

But on page 11 of the *Cleveland Plain Dealer* of May 24, 1957, is a picture of a man in a shirt and tie with a handful of slips of paper. He is peering into a large trunk containing a lot more of the same. Underneath is the caption: "'California Gold' Strike. Sgt. Carl J. Delau examines a trunkful of policy slips found in the home of Miss Dollree Mapp, ex-wife of boxer Jimmy Bivins and former girl friend of Archie Moore, light heavyweight champion of the world."

This is a continuation of a page-one story, which also says: "Ogletree, who had sneaked down the back stairs, was found in the downstairs home. A woman who lived there said he had threatened her." The newspaper account was confirmed much later by Miss Mapp herself, according to Fred W. Friendly and Martha J.H. Elliott, who interviewed her for their book *The Constitution: That Delicate Balance* (1984). They state: "Miss Mapp told the authors she knew Ogletree was downstairs." And in the original trial, defense witness Walter Greene gave the following information on cross-examination:

> *While you were out there, Mr. Green [sic], did you observe somebody being taken away from there?*
>
> Yes.
>
> *Do you know who it was?*
>
> There were two people.
>
> *Do you know who they were?*
>
> I know, of course, Mrs. Mapp, and I later learned the other was Virgil Ogletree. I saw him the first time in the downstairs suite.
>
> *On the first-floor suite?*
>
> Yes, ma'am.
>
> *And he was taken away in a patrol wagon?*
>
> That would be my best recollection.

Changing Stories

Let us be charitable and say that [defense attorneys] Mr. [Walter L.] Greene and his law partner A.L. Kearns expressed themselves oddly in their "Statement of the Case" three years later, when they said: "the police officers [were] frustrated in their attempt to find any individual involved in an extortion bombing."

The same is true with regard to the search warrant: "Upon demand of a search warrant, a piece of paper was held before the defendant without giving her an opportunity to view or read same. . . . This alleged search warrant was never proved or even tendered in the trial court upon request of the defendant." As to the first of those assertions, if you are confronted by a police officer in plain clothes and you question his identity, he will hold his credentials up in front of your eyes. He will not hand them to you, nor permit you to take them from him. This is standard police procedure. Before the advent of the Xerox process this same practice was followed with respect to warrants. With this in mind read the *Plain Dealer*'s description of the "fracas":

> . . . But not without one desperate last-ditch act of defiance from Miss Mapp. She met the policemen on the stairs. She grabbed the warrant from the hand of one of them.
>
> Then she stuffed it down the front of her dress. The raiders were startled, to say the least. But one of them rolled up a sleeve and said to her: "If you don't get it for us, I will." She returned the warrant.

Police reports made contemporaneously with the arrests confirm the existence of a search warrant. A report dated May 23, 1957, by Carl J. Delau states that the "subject would not come to the door but spoke to us through the second floor window. . . . Mapp stated that she would not let us in unless we had a search warrant. . . . Remained in the vicinity of this home until a search warrant obtained by Lieut. Thomas White who then came to this address. With the warrant in our possession we gained entrance. . . ." They found and seized "a large foot locker which contained considerable policy paraphernalia," "four books of a pornographic nature," and a "Colt make 'Bronco' automatic, 7.65(?), serial number 10410." Ogletree was found and arrested in the first-floor apartment. The tenant stated that she was "told by Mapp not to open the door for the police and for her to let Ogletree stay in her quarters."

Now a search warrant is not simply a piece of paper to be discarded when it has served its purpose. A police officer who obtains a warrant must "endorse" it and "return" it within a given time to the judicial authority that issued it. If the search warrant is executed, the "return" must be accompanied by an inventory of what was seized. All courts keep a copy and a record of the warrants they issue and all must be accounted for.

Mapp v. Ohio Lives On

The prosecution of Dollree Mapp for "Possession of Obscene Literature" in the Court of Common Pleas of Cuyahoga County was assigned Docket No. 68326. Many years ago, no one seems to know when, the case files for that year were microfilmed and thereafter destroyed. The files for the cases preceding 68326 are on microfilm in the office of the clerk of that court, as are the files for those that followed. Only No. 68326, *Ohio v. Mapp*, is missing. The only records that survive are those filed in the appeals to the Supreme Courts of Ohio and of the United States.

Three years later Mr. Kearns told the Supreme Court of the United States on oral argument:

> We asked during the trial of the case that the search warrant be produced and it was not.

> But the prosecutor promised—and we have the prosecutor here—that the search warrant would be produced and it never was.

If that is so further discussion is pointless. But in the *real* case of *Ohio v. Mapp*, the lieutenant, Thomas White, from whose hand Dollree Mapp snatched that "piece of paper," *was never asked anything by anybody*. The existence of a warrant to search the Mapp house was never once challenged at the original trial. Indeed, contrary to what Mr. Kearns told the Supreme Court, the defense *never* "asked during the trial of the case that the search warrant be produced," or at any other time either. The statements Mr. Kearns made to the Supreme Court of the United States were not just misleading, they were out and out lies.

Suppose they were? This case was decided thirty years ago; *Mapp v. Ohio* is *res judicata* [a settled matter]. True, but *Mapp v. Ohio* lives on, in the form of the exclusionary rule, under the doctrine of *stare decisis*, which makes each settled case a precedent for later ones.

But the validity of *stare decisis* depends on both sides of a legal argument being fairly and adequately represented by counsel. To suborn the selection or to collude or connive in the prosecution of a case strikes at the integrity of our jurisprudence. The question pressed here is whether the *Mapp v. Ohio* that affects our daily lives was a genuine "case or controversy" meeting these standards, or a sham, since

> an attempt, by a mere colorable dispute, to obtain the opinion of the court upon a question of law which a party desires to know for his own interest or his own purposes, when there is no real and substantial controversy between those who appear as adverse parties to the suit, is an abuse which courts of justice have always reprehended, and treated as a punishable contempt of court. *Lord v. Veazie*, 49 U.S. 251, 254 (1850). . . .

A Proper Warrant

On September 3, 1958, before the trial began, the defendant filed a "motion to suppress evidence." This is the way Mr. Kearns explained it to the trial court:

> Now we say that the State of Ohio did not have a search warrant setting forth the items that are mentioned in this indictment, which the State of Ohio intends to use in this case against this defendant, and for that reason we are asking that particular evidence be suppressed.

Note well this does not allege that the State of Ohio had no search warrant to search for Ogletree and policy slips. All Mr.

Kearns said was that there was no warrant *which specified* "lewd and lascivious Books, Pictures, and Photographs," and therefore that these could not be used in evidence. The trial judge overruled the motion and the trial began.

The prosecutor called only two witnesses, Patrolman Michael Haney and Sergeant Carl Delau. Both officers testified that they waited for about three hours until Lieutenant White arrived with what they assumed to be a warrant, although neither of them read it. Miss Mapp testified on her own behalf:

A. When they came in I said, "Inspector, I want to see the search warrant." . . .

He said, "Here is the search warrant." He held it back from me, and I remember Mr. Green told me that I should see it and read it, and I told him I wanted to see it. He said, "You can't see it." And then I reached over, took the search warrant from his hand and put it down in my bosom.

There is nothing suspicious about the testimony of Patrolman Haney or Sergeant Delau. When Lieutenant White appeared with the warrant there was no reason for him to show it to a junior officer. For either Haney or Delau to have asked to see it would have been quite out of line. Nor is there anything unusual about Miss Mapp's account. Lieutenant White held the search warrant up in front of her eyes close enough for her to be able to snatch it from him. If Lieutenant White did say, "You can't *see* it," he surely meant, "You can't *have* it," since he was holding it before her eyes.

Lieutenant White was not a witness to the discovery of the lewd literature. He could contribute nothing to the state's *prima facie* case. And the defense did not contend at the trial that the piece of paper Miss Mapp snatched from his hand was anything other than a search warrant. Under these circumstances there was absolutely no reason for the prosecution to call Lieutenant White.

Within the Law

Now, if the police had a warrant based upon "probable cause"—and under the circumstances we are entitled to assume that they did—they acted entirely within the law. The police couldn't *reasonably* search for Ogletree in a suitcase or a bureau drawer, but they could do so for policy slips; so, when they found the lewd booklets and a .25 caliber automatic pistol, these could lawfully be seized. It has been the law since the 1904 case of *Adams v. New York* that evidence found during the execution of an otherwise valid search is admissible whether specified in the warrant or not.

However, when Kearns and Greene took the case before the Cuyahoga Court of Appeals, they not only changed the grounds on which they argued, they also changed the facts of the case. And Mrs. [Gertrude Bower] Mahon [the assistant prosecutor]—the only person realistically in a position to refute their lies—disputed only inessentials, allowing them the point that really mattered.

They told the appeals court:

> There were from 7 to 12 police officers involved, they came according to Patrolman Haney to find some man for questioning as to a bombing, which some unknown said might be at the address. *No such man ever was there.* [Emphasis added.]

They painted the same picture to the Supreme Court of Ohio. Since "the alleged 'warrant' was never presented in evidence or shown to exist," said Kearns and Greene, "the conclusion was that the paper was a ruse. There was no proof of any 'person hiding out in her home who was wanted for questioning in connection with a . . . bombing'—that was a sham proposed to justify the inexcusable conduct of the officers in handcuffing her and going through the home of this mother and her young daughter."

Mrs. Mahon bravely challenged them on the number of police officers and the manner in which Miss Mapp was handcuffed. But she failed to point out that a bombing suspect *had* been found in Miss Mapp's home, as well as policy slips. Inexcusably she let pass her opponents' misrepresentations. However beastly the behavior of the Cleveland police, was her position, the smut seized had to be admitted as evidence because Ohio did not have the exclusionary rule.

Appealing to the Supreme Court

It was at this point that the real shell game was played. The appeal of *Ohio v. Mapp* was not decided on any search-and-seizure issue. The Ohio Supreme Court indeed found that Miss Mapp had been wrongly convicted—not because of anything to do with the exclusionary rule, but because the "lewd and lascivious materials" statute was "unconstitutionally invalid," since it placed an intolerable burden on the rights of free speech, press, and the dissemination of ideas protected as against the states by the Fourteenth Amendment. Ohio, however, had a provision in its own constitution, quite unique, stating that "No law shall be held unconstitutional and void by the Ohio Supreme Court without the concurrence of at least all but one of the judges." And in this case, "more than one of the judges of this court are of the opinion that no portion of the statute upon which defendant's conviction was based is unconstitutional." So, even though a majority of the Ohio Supreme Court found in Miss Mapp's favor, her conviction stood. And because the state court thus upheld a state statute against a claim that it violated the Constitution, Miss Mapp could appeal to the Supreme Court of the United States as a matter of right. *Mapp* could have happened "Only in Ohio."

On July 14, 1960, Kearns and Greene filed their Jurisdictional Statement in the United States Supreme Court. Here, as a general proposition, the appellant is required to show that the constitutional question he is now asking the Court to review was raised previously in the trial court. Here is how they fudged it: "The matter of the conduct of the police in procuring the evidence was first raised in the trial court in a 'Motion to Suppress' filed September 3, 1958." Of course, that motion said nothing of the sort. But again Mrs. Mahon let it pass— again inexcusably.

On October 24, 1960, the Supreme Court decided to hear the case of *Mapp v. Ohio*. Kearns and Greene filed their brief, essentially a rehash of the Jurisdictional Statement, on February 1, 1961. While the brief posed a search-and-seizure question, it was argued most perfunctorily. You cannot tell whether their position was that there was no warrant *at all*, or that the search was made pursuant to a warrant in which "obscene materials" were not specified. It is deliberately vague. . . .

The Decision

Mapp v. Ohio was argued on Wednesday, March 29, 1961. Mr. Kearns in his opening argument said:

> We asked during the trial of the case that the search warrant be produced and it was not.
>
> But the prosecutor promised—and we have the prosecutor here—that the search warrant would be produced, and it never was.

Moving along we see:

> *The Court*: Did you raise the question of no search warrant in the trial court?
>
> *Mr. Kearns*: I did. I even filed a motion to suppress the evidence in the trial court, which motion was overruled.

The ACLU's Mr. [Bernard] Berkman opened by saying he was "asking this Court to reconsider *Wolf v. Colorado* and to find that evidence which is unlawfully and illegally obtained should not be permitted into a state proceeding." The *amicus curiae* did not say how he arrived at the conclusion that any evidence against Miss Mapp was "unlawfully and illegally obtained." Aside from these remarks, his argument was directed toward the obvious unconstitutionality of the Ohio obscenity law.

This should not have distracted Mrs. Mahon. With respect to the search-and-seizure question her duty was clear. She was under an obligation to make absolutely certain the Court understood that: a) the bombing suspect and a trunk full of policy slips were found in Miss Mapp's house; b) the statements of the defense attorneys in this regard were false and misleading; c) the "motion to suppress evidence" made in the trial court did not place in issue the question of whether or not there existed a lawful warrant to search for Ogletree and "policy paraphernalia"; d) the defendant is therefore limited to asking the Court to reconsider the doctrine established in *Adams v. New York* that evidence incidentally found during an otherwise lawful search may be seized and used in court.

Mrs. Mahon did none of these things. Instead she merely repeated her assertion that "in the Ohio Constitution and under the Ohio laws, the fact that there was a search warrant would not make the evidence any the more competent or the fact that there was no search warrant would not make it any the less competent." That was a formulation that in effect endorsed the defense's account of the facts of the case.

On June 19, 1961, the Court handed down its decision. The constitutionality of the obscenity statute, the basis on which the case was briefed and argued, was airily dismissed in a footnote along with "other issues" not worthy of mention. While the decision did not get the headlines accorded the bomb blast which began this chain of events, *Mapp v. Ohio* nevertheless made the front pages of the Cleveland newspapers. The *Press & News* editorial saw it for exactly what it was:

A Landmark Decision

No one would have dreamed it, but a filthy book and picture case originating in Cleveland in 1957 has just resulted in a decision by the U.S. Supreme Court that will influence law enforcement all over the country.

. . . Sad to say, there were some sore losers. The National District Attorneys' Association filed an unsportsmanlike petition for a rehearing. It was denied October 9, 1961 (368 U.S. 871). Too late, I guess. If they wanted to appear *amicus curiae* they should have come forward earlier. But then maybe they thought it was a case involving free thought and expression.

But the ACLU's Bernard Berkman had a more accurate take on the case: "The decision in the *Mapp* case now prevents evidence obtained by official lawlessness from being used in a state court and we hope this ruling will deter official efforts in the future from obtaining evidence by unconstitutional methods." Or to translate Mr. Berkman's ACLU-speak, robbers, rapists, and murderers have now been loosed to prey upon society—with the unwitting acquiescence of the Supreme Court.

"Until . . . our society finally chooses to admit to and deal with the reality of unequal justice on the streets of America, the impact of Mapp will remain largely symbolic."

Mapp's Impact on the Black Community Has Been Mixed

Lewis R. Katz

In the following selection Lewis R. Katz examines the impact of the Mapp v. Ohio *decision on the African American community. Katz contends that at the time of the ruling, the early 1960s, blacks were routinely mistreated by police officers in various ways, including being subjected to unfair searches. The* Mapp *decision was thus part of a larger effort to correct the unfair treatment of African Americans. While he hails the* Mapp *decision as a positive development, Katz maintains that subsequent decisions have weakened its impact by allowing exceptions to search and seizure rules, allowing police officers greater flexibility in stopping and searching suspects. These exceptions have disproportionately eroded the rights of African Americans. However, despite the wakening of its precedent, Katz concludes,* Mapp *stands as a symbolic reminder that in order to protect liberty, it is necessary to allow some guilty suspects to go free.*

Katz, a professor at Case Western University School of Law, specializes in the Fourth Amendment. He has written extensively on the subject of search and seizure cases as well as other areas of criminal law.

Lewis R. Katz, "*Mapp* After 40 Years: Its Impact on Race in America," *Case Western Reserve Law Review*, vol. 52, 2001, pp. 471–87. Copyright © 2001 by *Case Western Reserve Law Review*. Reproduced by permission of the Copyright Clearance Center, Inc.

The facts in *Mapp v. Ohio* were not unusual. White plain-clothes police officers, looking for a man suspected of bombing Don King's home, surrounded Dollree Mapp's house, an African-American woman known to the police, when the suspect's car was found parked outside the house. They knocked on the door, but Mapp denied them entrance without a search warrant. The officers radioed for a warrant, but presumably without waiting for one, detectives accompanied by six uniformed officers broke out the front glass of the door, entered, and searched the house. The lead detective told her he had a warrant and waved a piece of paper in her face, a paper which she allegedly grabbed and stuffed in her blouse. After handcuffing Mapp, the officers retrieved the paper, but no warrant was offered at a trial. While the suspect was not found in the house, the officers found pencil sketches of male and female nudes packed in a box and suitcase in Mapp's bedroom. Mapp was charged with possession of obscene materials, a felony. Even if there had been a warrant to search for the suspected bomber, it would not have extended to a box and suitcase in which he could not have been hiding. . . .

Impact on the Black Community

The impact of *Mapp* was naturally greatest in the African-American community where Fourth Amendment violations were the most common. Whatever limited effect *Mapp* would have, it would be felt most where police conduct was the least restrained. It was this community which the Warren Court [the U.S. Supreme Court under Chief Justice Earl Warren, 1953–1969] intended to benefit by the due process revolution, because wherever injustice existed in America, its worst impact was felt in the black community.

The *Mapp* decision went hand-in-hand with *Brown v. Board of Education* and other decisions of the Warren Court seeking to eliminate legal barriers to racial justice. In *Brown* it was the laws that mandated racial segregation; in *Mapp* it was the underlying law enforcement culture in the country that tolerated and encouraged police to treat African-Americans and other racial minorities differently from the majority population. And different meant worse. The police were not unique in this regard; they were part of the racist culture that permeated American life and that has not yet disappeared. The impact of the racist culture on relations between police and African-Americans is readily apparent throughout American history. The white police officers who invaded Dollree Mapp's home did so with confidence that they would not be called to task for violating her fundamental rights by entering her home without a warrant. How the police behaved in Dollree Mapp's house was consistent with historical practice in the United States.

History of Law Enforcement and African-Americans

Since before the founding of the Republic, law enforcement officers were used primarily to track the movements of African-Americans and to ensure their subservience. Prior to the Civil War, it mattered little whether the African-American was a slave or a freeman. Sheriffs and other law enforcement officers treated them the same, thereby reducing the Negro freeman to slave status in the eyes of the law. The Civil War changed little in that regard. In the South, after Reconstruction precipitously ended, sheriffs and their deputies, as well as police in the cities, were the instrument of repression, working hand-in-hand with nightriders who would keep the African-American population terrorized and subservient. Police failed to prevent lynchings or apprehend the perpetrators.

Even in the North, the African-American population received very different justice on the street than whites. While relations between police and all citizens on the street during the first six decades of the twentieth century were rough and characterized by arbitrary overreaching by police, the full brunt of police lawlessness and brutality fell on the African-American community. Arbitrarily stopping and detaining African-Americans, engaging in dragnet arrests of African-Americans, and, as in the *Mapp* case, entering homes without warrants, police ensured that African-Americans were second-class citizens, receiving rougher justice than that accorded the rest of the population. Police brutality towards African-Americans was as common in the North as in the South. And the criminal justice system, then as now, meted out disproportionately harsher penalties to African-American defendants than it did to white defendants.

The Warren Court Sought to Correct Past Injustices

The Warren Court's due process revolution sought to achieve a more level playing field in state criminal proceedings by applying the procedural guarantees of the Bill of Rights to state criminal cases. *Mapp* also sought to achieve justice on the streets by imposing the exclusionary rule on state criminal proceedings to discourage police from violating Fourth Amendment rights.

Whatever effect *Mapp* may have had on the streets immediately after 1961, that effect was, at the very least, diminished after 1968. In 1968, the same Warren Court, in *Terry v. Ohio*, reacting to growing national concern about increases in crime, sanctioned seizures of the person on less than probable cause required for arrest. The *Terry* investigative stop requires a lesser standard than probable cause, namely reasonable suspicion, to justify an investigative detention. Moreover, in the hands of a Supreme Court less sensitive to minority concerns during the subsequent thirty years, the *Terry* stop, which the Warren Court acknowledged is a Fourth Amendment seizure, grew in its impact on the African-American community. The area in which a stop takes place, such as a "high-crime area," became a factor in determining the reasonableness of a stop, thereby making inner-city residents far more subject to these stops than other citizens. While race is not a constitutionally acceptable factor in determining reasonableness, and thus the legitimacy of the investigative stop, "high crime area" often is a euphemism for race, legitimizing race as a consideration.

Was *Terry* a Step Backward?

No one knows, for certain, whether the decision in *Terry* represented a loss of courage and commitment by the Warren Court to equal justice on the streets. These stops, though illegal, were common prior to the Court's decision in *Terry*. The Court may have legitimized them in order to get control by putting them within the framework of the Fourth Amendment. However, the cost of providing this tool to help law enforcement prevent crime has grown over the years. The momentary detention allowed and envisaged by Chief Justice Warren in *Terry* has grown under the Burger and Rehnquist Courts to allow for longer detentions and the use of substantial force absent probable cause to justify a full-fledged arrest.

Worse, the later Courts narrowed the category of *Terry* stop by expanding another category, "consensual encounters" between police and citizens, which implicate no Fourth Amendment rights and, thus, provide for no Fourth Amendment oversight of the reasonableness of the police conduct. The "consensual encounter" is predicated upon the Supreme Court's conclusion that no reasonable innocent person would believe that he is not free to leave rather than comply with a police officer's request that the person stop and provide information, even though it is patently obvious that no reasonable innocent person, not schooled in the fine points of Fourth Amendment jurisprudence, would feel free to disregard a police officer under most of these circumstances. It is little wonder, then, that issues such as racial profiling have reached the political radar. Racial profiling by police is an issue that actually predates the founding of the Republic, but it has become such a wide-spread negation of basic Fourth Amendment rights that its existence imperils not only the people who are subject to such interference because of race or ethnicity but the liberty of all Americans. If the nation continues to disregard, and thus ratify, this injustice, it raises questions about the security of all Americans from unreasonable searches and seizures.

Muting *Mapp*'s Message

By controlling movement, you control behavior. *Mapp* essentially protects freedom of movement from unreasonable interference by police. By making unreasonable interference with the movement of African-Americans, like all Americans, costly to the government by denying it the use of evidence found during such interference, *Mapp* helped to promote the freedom of movement for all Americans. However, *Mapp* especially promoted the freedom of movement for African-Americans who were subject to harassment and other unreasonable interference more than most Americans. *Terry* and its progeny expanded the opportunities for police interference with African-Americans' freedom of movement. It further expanded police interference by allowing the area where a stop takes place to be a positive factor in determining the reasonableness of a stop. This increases the opportunities for stops in the inner cities, where most people stopped will be African-Americans or other minorities. While the courts say "area" alone is not enough, area "alone" is often coupled with other, innocuous factors. The net result is subjecting people in the inner cities, most of whom are not and have never been involved in criminal activity, to constant police interference in their movements in ways, degrees, and frequency unknown by the rest of America. The *Terry* stop, and its expansion, as well as the expansion of unregulated consensual encounters, has muted *Mapp*'s message, especially on the streets of inner-city communities where African-Americans continue to be stopped and hassled by police much more so than in other communities. It is not surprising that the message has been muted. The Warren Court saw the need to ensure the quality of justice for those in this country who were denied it. The successor Courts have not been attuned to this need but, instead, have used their powers to accommodate law enforcement convenience by expanding police authority to intervene without prior judicial authorization and without exigent circumstances, which traditionally provided the justification for warrantless intrusions.

A Step in the Right Direction

It would be wrong for the reader to conclude that I think that *Mapp* after forty years has made little difference in the due process equation. The rule in *Mapp* continues to be enforced most fully when the police intrusion takes place in a home, which is precisely the fact situation presented in *Mapp v. Ohio*. The Supreme Court, even the post-Warren Court, zealously protects the Fourth Amendment rights of Americans in their homes, except when it comes to allowing the prosecution to use evidence secured with an illegal search warrant that was "reasonably relied upon" by the police.

It is on the streets of America where the message of *Mapp* has been muted. Nonetheless, despite the continued lack of equal justice on the streets and the weakening of the protections of the exclusionary rule, and consequently the weakening of Fourth Amendment rights outside of the home, *Mapp* continues to have symbolic effect. Every time a court rules that reliable and relevant evidence of guilt must be suppressed, resulting sometimes in the dismissal of charges against a likely guilty defendant, we are reminded that the cost of maintaining individual liberties is substantial. *Mapp* made us confront those costs on a regular basis in every court in the land. It makes us reaffirm our commitment to liberty in a tough, tangible way.

Someday a future Supreme Court—now farther than ever in the future—must confront the costs to liberty of the dilution of *Mapp* and the resulting expansion of police power, especially as a result of the "war on drugs." Until that day, when our society finally chooses to admit to and deal with the reality of unequal justice on the streets of America, the impact of *Mapp* will remain largely symbolic.

Securing the
Right Against
Self-Incrimination

Case Overview

Miranda v. Arizona (1966)

Miranda v. Arizona established the now-famous Miranda rights. The Supreme Court ruled that upon arrest and before being questioned, suspects must be made aware of their Fifth and Sixth Amendment rights. These rights include the right to remain silent, to have an attorney present during questioning, and to have an attorney provided by the state if the suspect cannot afford one.

The case involved Ernesto Miranda, who in March 1963 was arrested for kidnapping and raping a young woman as she walked home from the movies. Miranda was picked out of a lineup by the victim, and, after being interrogated for two hours by the police, he confessed. He provided a written statement and signed a typed document stating that he understood his rights against self-incrimination and was waiving them.

Miranda's case was brought to trial with only his confession entered into evidence. His lawyer fought to have the confession thrown out, stating that Miranda did not have a lawyer present and did not fully understand his rights at the time he confessed. Miranda was convicted of kidnapping and rape and sentenced to twenty to thirty years in prison for each count. His attorney appealed to the Arizona Supreme Court. During this trial the police officers that had interrogated Miranda admitted that they had not advised him of his rights. However, the Arizona court upheld the conviction. The case was presented to the Supreme Court in 1966.

On June 13, 1966, the Court, in a 5-4 decision, overturned Miranda's conviction, stating that the police must do everything they can to make sure suspects are aware of their rights under the Constitution. The Fifth Amendment states that suspects are not to be compelled to incriminate themselves. The

Supreme Court ruling in *Brown v. Mississippi* (1936) had strengthened the Fifth Amendment by stating that a suspect could not be forced to confess. The Sixth Amendment states that all suspects have the right to have counsel present while on trial. In the 1963 decision of *Gideon v. Wainwright*, the Court had extended this right, stating that if the suspect could not afford a lawyer, one would be provided by the government. The Court decided that Miranda had not been made aware of these rights and thus his confession was coerced and invalid.

The Court also declared that the typed statement by which Miranda waived his rights was improper because it was signed after the confession was given. In its ruling the Court created a procedure that would govern both informing suspects of their rights as well as how those rights could be waived. To accomplish this the Court established the Miranda warnings, a series of statements that were to be read to every suspect placed in police custody prior to questioning.

In the 2000 case of *Dickerson v. United States* the Supreme Court affirmed the *Miranda* ruling. Congress had passed a law allowing courts to admit a confession as evidence if the suspect had not been read his Miranda rights but had confessed voluntarily. The Court rejected this effort to legislatively overrule *Miranda*, declaring that "the [*Miranda*] warnings have become part of our national culture."

"In order to ... permit a full opportunity to exercise the privilege against self-incrimination, the accused must be adequately and effectively apprised of his rights."

The Court's Decision: Suspects' Fifth Amendment Rights Must Be Defended

Earl Warren

Earl Warren served as chief justice of the Supreme Court from 1953 to 1969. During his time on the Court he oversaw many landmark civil rights cases, including Brown v. Board of Education, *which mandated the desegregation of public schools.*

The following selection is excerpted from the majority opinion in Miranda v. Arizona, *which Warren wrote. The ruling established procedures that must be followed in order to protect the rights of suspects against self-incrimination during questioning by police. Specifically, suspects must be informed that they have the right to remain silent, that any statement they make can and will be used against them, that they have the right to have an attorney present during questioning, and to have an attorney provided for them if they cannot afford one. These guidelines became known as the Miranda rights. Unless a suspect is informed of these rights, the Court concluded, any statement the suspect makes in response to police questioning cannot be used in court.*

There can be no doubt that the Fifth Amendment privilege is available outside of criminal court proceedings and

Earl Warren, majority opinion, *Miranda v. Arizona*, June 13, 1966.

serves to protect persons in all settings in which their freedom of action is curtailed in any significant way from being compelled to incriminate themselves. We have concluded that without proper safeguards the process of in-custody interrogation of persons suspected or accused of crime contains inherently compelling pressures which work to undermine the individual's will to resist and to compel him to speak where he would not otherwise do so freely. In order to combat these pressures and to permit a full opportunity to exercise the privilege against self-incrimination, the accused must be adequately and effectively apprised of his rights and the exercise of those rights must be fully honored. . . .

We encourage Congress and the States to continue their laudable search for increasingly effective ways of protecting the rights of the individual while promoting efficient enforcement of our criminal laws. However, unless we are shown other procedures which are at least as effective in apprising accused persons of their right of silence and in assuring a continuous opportunity to exercise it, the following safeguards must be observed.

The Right to Remain Silent

At the outset, if a person in custody is to be subjected to interrogation, he must first be informed in clear and unequivocal terms that he has the right to remain silent. For those unaware of the privilege, the warning is needed simply to make them aware of it—the threshold requirement for an intelligent decision as to its exercise. More important, such a warning is an absolute prerequisite in overcoming the inherent pressures of the interrogation atmosphere. It is not just the subnormal or woefully ignorant who succumb to an interrogator's imprecations, whether implied or expressly stated, that the interrogation will continue until a confession is obtained or that silence in the face of accusation is itself damning and will bode ill when presented to a jury. Further, the warning will show the individual that his interrogators are prepared to recognize his privilege should he choose to exercise it.

The Fifth Amendment privilege is so fundamental to our system of constitutional rule and the expedient of giving an adequate warning as to the availability of the privilege so simple, we will not pause to inquire in individual cases whether the defendant was aware of his rights without a warning being given. Assessments of the knowledge the defendant possessed, based on information as to his age, education, intelligence, or prior contact with authorities, can never be more than speculation; a warning is a clearcut fact. More important, whatever the background of the person interrogated, a warning at the time of the interrogation is indispensable to overcome its pressures and to insure that the individual knows he is free to exercise the privilege at that point in time.

The warning of the right to remain silent must be accompanied by the explanation that anything said can and will be used against the individual in court. This warning is needed in order to make him aware not only of the privilege, but also of the consequences of forgoing it. It is only through an awareness of these consequences that there can be any assurance of real understanding and intelligent exercise of the privilege. Moreover, this warning may serve to make the individual more acutely aware that he is faced with a phase of the adversary system—that he is not in the presence of persons acting solely in his interest.

The Right to Have Counsel Present

The circumstances surrounding in-custody interrogation can operate very quickly to overbear the will of one merely made aware of his privilege by his interrogators. Therefore, the right to have counsel present at the interrogation is indispensable to the protection of the Fifth Amendment privilege under the system we delineate today. Our aim is to assure that the individual's right to choose between silence and speech remains unfettered throughout the interrogation process. A once-stated warning, delivered by those who will conduct the interrogation, cannot itself suffice to that end among those who most require knowledge of their rights. A mere warning given by the interrogators is not alone sufficient to accomplish that end. . . . Even preliminary advice given to the accused by his own attorney can be swiftly overcome by the secret interrogation process. Thus, the need for counsel to protect the Fifth Amendment privilege comprehends not merely a right to consult with counsel prior to questioning, but also to have counsel present during any questioning if the defendant so desires.

The presence of counsel at the interrogation may serve several significant subsidiary functions as well. If the accused decides to talk to his interrogators, the assistance of counsel can mitigate the dangers of untrustworthiness. With a lawyer present the likelihood that the police will practice coercion is reduced, and if coercion is nevertheless exercised the lawyer can testify to it in court. The presence of a lawyer can also help to guarantee that the accused gives a fully accurate statement to the police and that the statement is rightly reported by the prosecution at trial.

Failure to Request Counsel Is Not a Waiver

An individual need not make a pre-interrogation request for a lawyer. While such request affirmatively secures his right to have one, his failure to ask for a lawyer does not constitute a waiver. No effective waiver of the right to counsel during interrogation can be recognized unless specifically made after the warnings we here delineate have been given. The accused who does not know his rights and therefore does not make a request may be the person who most needs counsel. . . .

Accordingly we hold that an individual held for interrogation must be clearly informed that he has the right to consult with a lawyer and to have the lawyer with him during interrogation under the system for protecting the privilege we delineate today. As with the warnings of the right to remain silent and that anything stated can be used in evidence against him, this warning is an absolute prerequisite to interrogation. No amount of circumstantial evidence that the person may have been aware of this right will suffice to stand in its stead: Only through such a warning is there ascertainable assurance that the accused was aware of this right.

An Attorney Must Be Provided

If an individual indicates that he wishes the assistance of counsel before any interrogation occurs, the authorities cannot rationally ignore or deny his request on the basis that the individual does not have or cannot afford a retained attorney. The financial ability of the individual has no relationship to the scope of the rights involved here. The privilege against self-incrimination secured by the Constitution applies to all individuals. The need for counsel in order to protect the privilege exists for the indigent as well as the affluent. In fact, were we to limit these constitutional rights to those who can retain an attorney, our decisions today would be of little significance. The cases before us as well as the vast majority of confession cases with which we have dealt in the past involve those unable to retain counsel. While authorities are not required to relieve the accused of his poverty, they have the obligation not to take advantage of indigence in the administration of justice. Denial of counsel to the indigent at the time of interrogation while allowing an attorney to those who can afford one would be no more supportable by reason or logic than the similar situation at trial and on appeal struck down in *Gideon v. Wainwright* (1963) and *Douglas v. California* (1963).

In order fully to apprise a person interrogated of the extent of his rights under this system then, it is necessary to warn him not only that he has the right to consult with an attorney, but also that if he is indigent a lawyer will be appointed to represent him. Without this additional warning, the admonition of the right to consult with counsel would often be understood as meaning only that he can consult with a lawyer if he has one or has the funds to obtain one. The warning of a right to counsel would be hollow if not couched in terms that would convey to the indigent—the person most often subjected to interrogation—the knowledge that he too has a right to have counsel present. As with the warnings of the right to remain silent and of the general right to counsel, only by effective and express explanation to the indigent of this right can there be assurance that he was truly in a position to exercise it.

Results of Warnings

Once warnings have been given, the subsequent procedure is clear. If the individual indicates in any manner, at any time prior to or during questioning, that he wishes to remain silent, the interrogation must cease. At this point he has shown that he intends to exercise his Fifth Amendment privilege; any statement taken after the person invokes his privilege cannot be other than the product of compulsion, subtle or otherwise. Without the right to cut off questioning, the setting of in-custody interrogation operates on the individual to overcome free choice in producing a statement after the privilege has been once invoked. If the individual states that he wants an attorney, the interrogation must cease until an attorney is present. At that time, the individual must have an opportunity to confer with the attorney and to have him present during any subsequent questioning. If the individual cannot obtain an attorney and he indicates that he wants one before speaking to police, they must respect his decision to remain silent.

This does not mean, as some have suggested, that each police station must have a "station house lawyer" present at all times to advise prisoners. It does mean, however, that if police propose to interrogate a person they must make known to him that he is entitled to a lawyer and that if he cannot afford one, a lawyer will be provided for him prior to any interrogation. If authorities conclude that they will not provide counsel during a reasonable period of time in which investigation in the field is carried out, they may refrain from doing so without violating the person's Fifth Amendment privilege so long as they do not question him during that time.

If the interrogation continues without the presence of an attorney and a statement is taken, a heavy burden rests on the government to demonstrate that the defendant knowingly and intelligently waived his privilege against self-incrimination and his right to retained or appointed counsel. This Court has always set high standards of proof for the waiver of constitutional rights, and we re-assert these standards as applied to in-custody interrogation. Since the State is responsible for establishing the isolated circumstances under which the interrogation takes place and has the only means of making available corroborated evidence of warnings given during incommunicado interrogation, the burden is rightly on its shoulders.

Procedures When Suspects Waive Rights

An express statement that the individual is willing to make a statement and does not want an attorney followed closely by a statement could constitute a waiver. But a valid waiver will not be presumed simply from the silence of the accused after warnings are given or simply from the fact that a confession was in fact eventually obtained. . . .

Moreover, where in-custody interrogation is involved, there is no room for the contention that the privilege is waived if the individual answers some questions or gives some information on his own prior to invoking his right to remain silent when interrogated.

Whatever the testimony of the authorities as to waiver of rights by an accused, the fact of lengthy interrogation or incommunicado incarceration before a statement is made is strong evidence that the accused did not validly waive his rights. In these circumstances the fact that the individual eventually made a statement is consistent with the conclusion that the compelling influence of the interrogation finally forced him to do so. It is inconsistent with any notion of a voluntary relinquishment of the privilege. Moreover, any evidence that the accused was threatened, tricked, or cajoled into a waiver will, of course, show that the defendant did not voluntarily waive his privilege. The requirement of warnings and waiver of rights is a fundamental with respect to the Fifth Amendment privilege and not simply a preliminary ritual to existing methods of interrogation. . . .

The Effect on Police Work

Our decision is not intended to hamper the traditional function of police officers in investigating crime. When an individual is in custody on probable cause, the police may, of course, seek out evidence in the field to be used at trial against him. Such investigation may include inquiry of persons not under restraint. General on-the-scene questioning as to facts surrounding a crime or other general questioning of citizens in the fact-finding process is not affected by our holding. It is an act of responsible citizenship for individuals to give whatever information they may have to aid in law enforcement. In such situations the compelling atmosphere inherent in the process of in-custody interrogation is not necessarily present.

In dealing with statements obtained through interrogation, we do not purport to find all confessions inadmissible. Confessions remain a proper element in law enforcement. Any statement given freely and voluntarily without any compelling influences is, of course, admissible in evidence. The fundamental import of the privilege while an individual is in custody is not whether he is allowed to talk to the police without the benefit of warnings and counsel, but whether he can be interrogated. There is no requirement that police stop a person who enters a police station and states that he wishes to confess to a crime, or a person who calls the police to offer a confession or any other statement he desires to make. Volunteered statements of any kind are not barred by the Fifth Amendment and their admissibility is not affected by our holding today.

To summarize, we hold that when an individual is taken into custody or otherwise deprived of his freedom by the authorities in any significant way and is subjected to questioning, the privilege against self-incrimination is jeopardized. Procedural safeguards must be employed to protect the privilege, and unless other fully effective means are adopted to notify the person of his right of silence and to assure that the exercise of the right will be scrupulously honored, the following measures are required. He must be warned prior to any questioning that he has the right to remain silent, that anything he says can be used against him in a court of law, that he has the right to the presence of an attorney, and that if he cannot afford an attorney one will be appointed for him prior to any questioning if he so desires. Opportunity to exercise these rights must be afforded to him throughout the interrogation. After such warnings have been given, and such opportunity afforded him, the individual may knowingly and intelligently waive these rights and agree to answer questions or make a statement. But unless and until such warnings and waiver are demonstrated by the prosecution at trial, no evidence obtained as a result of interrogation can be used against him.

> "The Court is taking a real risk with
> society's welfare in imposing its new
> regime on the country."

Dissenting Opinion: *Miranda* Is Unnecessary and Damaging to Law Enforcement

John Marshall Harlan II

The following selection is an excerpt from the dissenting opinion of John Marshall Harlan II in the Supreme Court case of Miranda v. Arizona. *In that case the Court overturned the conviction of Ernesto Miranda for kidnapping and rape on the grounds that his confession had been coerced. The Court also established strict procedures that must be followed to obtain a legitimate confession that can be used in court.*

In his dissent Harlan contends that Miranda *will not curtail dubious police practices. Officers who are inclined to use improper interrogation techniques will not be deterred by the new rules. Rather, Harlan insists,* Miranda *will simply undermine the effectiveness of legitimate interrogations by eliminating all pressure on suspects and thereby discouraging confessions altogether. A guilty suspect, after being told that he is not required to speak and is entitled to a lawyer, will be unlikely to confess, argues Harlan.*

Harlan was the grandson of a Supreme Court justice and served on the Court himself from 1955 until his death on December 30, 1971.

I believe the decision of the Court represents poor constitutional law and entails harmful consequences for the coun-

John Marshall Harlan II, dissenting opinion, *Miranda v. Arizona*, June 13, 1966.

try at large. How serious these consequences may prove to be only time can tell. But the basic flaws in the Court's justification seem to me readily apparent now once all sides of the problem are considered.

At the outset, it is well to note exactly what is required by the Court's new constitutional code of rules for confessions. The foremost requirement, upon which later admissibility of a confession depends, is that a fourfold warning be given to a person in custody before he is questioned; namely, that he has a right to remain silent, that anything he says may be used against him, that he has a right to have present an attorney during the questioning, and that if indigent he has a right to a lawyer without charge. To forgo these rights, some affirmative statement of rejection is seemingly required, and threats, tricks, or cajolings to obtain this waiver are forbidden. If before or during questioning the suspect seeks to invoke his right to remain silent, interrogation must be forgone or cease; a request for counsel brings about the same result until a lawyer is procured. Finally, there are a miscellany of minor directives, for example, the burden of proof of waiver is on the State, admissions and exculpatory statements are treated just like confessions, withdrawal of a waiver is always permitted, and so forth.

Voluntariness with a Vengeance

While the fine points of this scheme are far less clear than the Court admits, the tenor is quite apparent. The new rules are not designed to guard against police brutality or other unmistakably banned forms of coercion. Those who use third-degree tactics and deny them in court are equally able and destined to lie as skillfully about warnings and waivers. Rather, the thrust of the new rules is to negate all pressures, to reinforce the nervous or ignorant suspect, and ultimately to discourage any confession at all. The aim in short is toward "voluntariness" in a utopian sense, or to view it from a different angle, voluntariness with a vengeance.

To incorporate this notion into the Constitution requires a strained reading of history and precedent and a disregard of the very pragmatic concerns that alone may on occasion justify such strains. I believe that reasoned examination will show that the Due Process Clauses provide an adequate tool for coping with confessions and that, even if the Fifth Amendment privilege against self-incrimination be invoked, its precedents taken as a whole do not sustain the present rules. Viewed as a choice based on pure policy, these new rules prove to be a highly debatable, if not one-sided, appraisal of the competing interests, imposed over widespread objection, at the very time when judicial restraint is most called for by the circumstances. . . .

The Court Has Changed Interrogation

Examined as an expression of public policy, the Court's new regime proves so dubious that there can be no due compensation for its weakness in constitutional law. The Court [is mistaken] in implying that the Constitution has struck the balance in favor of the approach the Court takes. Rather, precedent reveals that the Fourteenth Amendment in practice has been construed to strike a different balance, that the Fifth Amendment gives the Court little solid support in this context, and that the Sixth Amendment should have no bearing at all. Legal history has been stretched before to satisfy deep needs of society. In this instance, however, the Court has not and cannot make the powerful showing that its new rules are plainly desirable in the context of our society, something which is surely demanded before those rules are engrafted onto the Constitution and imposed on every State and county in the land.

Without at all subscribing to the generally black picture of police conduct painted by the Court, I think it must be frankly recognized at the outset that police questioning allowable under due process precedents may inherently entail some pressure on the suspect and may seek advantage in his ignorance or weaknesses. The atmosphere and questioning techniques, proper and fair though they be, can in themselves exert a tug on the suspect to confess, and in this light "to speak of any confessions of crime made after arrest as being 'voluntary' or 'uncoerced' is somewhat inaccurate, although traditional. A confession is wholly and incontestably voluntary only if a guilty person gives himself up to the law and becomes his own accuser." *Ashcraft v. Tennessee*. Until today, the role of the Constitution has been only to sift out undue pressure, not to assure spontaneous confessions.

The Court's new rules aim to offset these minor pressures and disadvantages intrinsic to any kind of police interrogation. The rules do not serve due process interests in preventing blatant coercion since . . . they do nothing to contain the policeman who is prepared to lie from the start. The rules work for reliability in confessions almost only in the . . . sense that they can prevent some from being given at all. In short, the benefit of this new regime is simply to lessen or wipe out the inherent compulsion and inequalities to which the Court devotes some nine pages of description.

The Decision Hampers Law Enforcement

What the Court largely ignores is that its rules impair, if they will not eventually serve wholly to frustrate, an instrument of law enforcement that has long and quite reasonably been thought worth the price paid for it. There can be little doubt that the Court's new code would markedly decrease the number of confessions. To warn the suspect that he may remain silent and remind him that his confession may be used in court are minor obstructions. To require also an express waiver by the suspect and an end to questioning whenever he demurs must heavily handicap questioning. And to suggest or provide counsel for the suspect simply invites the end of the interrogation.

How much harm this decision will inflict on law enforcement cannot fairly be predicted with accuracy. Evidence on the role of confessions is notoriously incomplete, and little is added by the Court's reference to the FBI experience and the resources believed wasted in interrogation. We do know that some crimes cannot be solved without confessions, that ample expert testimony attests to their importance in crime control, and that the Court is taking a real risk with society's welfare in imposing its new regime on the country. The social costs of crime are too great to call the new rules anything but a hazardous experimentation.

While passing over the costs and risks of its experiment, the Court portrays the evils of normal police questioning in terms which I think are exaggerated. Albeit stringently confined by the due process standards interrogation is no doubt often inconvenient and unpleasant for the suspect. However, it is no less so for a man to be arrested and jailed, to have his house searched, or to stand trial in court, yet all this may properly happen to the most innocent given probable cause, a warrant, or an indictment. Society has always paid a stiff price for law and order, and peaceful interrogation is not one of the dark moments of the law.

The Facts of the Case

This brief statement of the competing considerations seems to me ample proof that the Court's preference is highly debatable at best and therefore not to be read into the Constitution. However, it may make the analysis more graphic to consider the actual facts of one of the four cases reversed by the Court. *Miranda v. Arizona* serves best, being neither the hardest nor easiest of the four under the Court's standards.

On March 3, 1963, an 18-year-old girl was kidnapped and forcibly raped near Phoenix, Arizona. Ten days later, on the morning of March 13, petitioner Miranda was arrested and taken to the police station. At this time Miranda was 23 years old, indigent, and educated to the extent of completing half the ninth grade. He had "an emotional illness" of the schizophrenic type, according to the doctor who eventually examined him; the doctor's report also stated that Miranda was "alert and oriented as to time, place, and person," intelligent within normal limits, competent to stand trial, and sane within the legal definition. At the police station, the victim picked Miranda out of a lineup, and two officers then took him into a separate room to interrogate him, starting about 11:30 A.M. Though at first denying his guilt, within a short time Miranda gave a detailed oral confession and then wrote out in his own hand and signed a brief statement admitting and describing the crime. All this was accomplished in two hours or less without any force, threats or promises and—I will assume this though the record is uncertain—without any effective warnings at all.

Miranda's oral and written confessions are now held inadmissible under the Court's new rules. One is entitled to feel astonished that the Constitution can be read to produce this result. These confessions were obtained during brief, daytime questioning conducted by two officers and unmarked by any of the traditional indicia of coercion. They assured a conviction for a brutal and unsettling crime, for which the police had and quite possibly could obtain little evidence other than the victim's identifications, evidence which is frequently unreliable. There was, in sum, a legitimate purpose, no perceptible unfairness, and certainly little risk of injustice in the interrogation. Yet the resulting confessions, and the responsible course of police practice they represent, are to be sacrificed to the Court's own finespun conception of fairness which I seriously doubt is shared by many thinking citizens in this country. . . .

In conclusion: Nothing in the letter or the spirit of the Constitution or in the precedents squares with the heavy-handed and one-sided action that is so precipitously taken by the Court in the name of fulfilling its constitutional responsibilities. The foray which the Court makes today brings to mind the wise and farsighted words of Mr. Justice [Robert H.] Jackson in *Douglas v. Jeannette*: "This Court is forever adding new stories to the temples of constitutional law, and the temples have a way of collapsing when one story too many is added."

"The police and prosecutors should reconsider their Miranda practices."

Excessive Application of *Miranda* Has Hampered Police Work

Fred E. Inbau

Fred E. Inbau, who died in 1998, taught law at Northwestern University in Evanston, Illinois. Inbau specialized in criminal justice, particularly in the area of police interrogation. He believed that the police should have broader powers in order to prevent crime rather than simply react to it. He founded Americans for Effective Law Enforcement (AELE) to support the efforts of the police and to petition the courts on their behalf.

In the following selection Inbau argues that police and prosecutors are overapplying the Miranda rules. Those rules require police to inform suspects of four rights related to interrogation and counsel. When suspects waive these rights, any statements they make can be used against them in court. According to Inbau, police and prosecutors are so fearful of having their suspects' confessions deemed inadmissible that they are exceeding the Court's mandate in Miranda v. Arizona. For example, in some cases they are obtaining written waivers and informing suspects of a fifth right that they are not required to state. These extra efforts are unnecessary and simply lessen their chances of obtaining a confession, Inbau concludes.

Fred E. Inbau, "Over-Reaction—The Mischief of *Miranda v. Arizona*," *The Journal of Criminal Law & Criminology*, vol. 73, 1982, pp. 1,451–53, 1,455–58, 1,463–64. Copyright © 1982 by the Northwestern University School of Law. Reproduced by permission.

Immediately after the attempted assassination of President Ronald Reagan in Washington, D.C., on the early afternoon of March 30, 1981, Secret Service agents and the District of Columbia police arrested John W. Hinckley, Jr. and took him to the local police headquarters, arriving there at 2:40 P.M. They wanted to question Hinckley not only as to his motive but also about the possible involvement of accomplices. Before doing so, however, they dutifully read to him the warnings of constitutional rights that the Supreme Court in 1966 mandated in its five-to-four decision in *Miranda v. Arizona*. The warnings given to Hinckley, as we shall see, contained embellishments of the ones specified in *Miranda*, and they were read to him on *three separate occasions* within a *two hour period*. After receiving the third set of warnings Hinckley was presented with a "waiver of rights" form on which he responded "yes" to the questions whether he had read his rights and understood them. Then he was asked whether he "wished to answer any questions." At this point Hinckley answered, "I don't know. I'm not sure; I think I ought to talk to Joe Bates [his father's lawyer in Dallas]." Hinckley added: "I want to talk to you, but first I want to talk to Joe Bates." . . .

Before proceeding to discuss several other cases to illustrate the mischief occasioned by *Miranda*, the writer reiterates that Hinckley had received the prescribed warnings *three* times within a two-hour interval, and that a *signed* waiver was sought from him at the D.C. police station when he was asked if he *wished* to answer any questions. Nowhere in the *Miranda* opinion is there anything requiring such a repetition of the warnings, or the need for a signed statement, or the ascertainment of any other kind of waiver than an indicated willingness to be questioned. Why, then, the mischief?

The mischief in the *Hinckley* case resulted from a concern on the part of law enforcement officers—and an understandable concern—that whatever they say to a suspect by way of *Miranda* requirements might later be considered inadequate by a judge or appellate court. Hence, they over-react; they embellish the warnings or add new ones. Each time someone wants to talk to the suspect, or the same interrogator wants to resume his interrogation, the warnings are repeated. The repetitive warnings are followed by a request to sign a legalistically shrouded waiver form. As a consequence of all of this, suspects who might otherwise have been willing to talk are far less apt to do so.

The *Alexander* Case

Another illustration of over-reaction to *Miranda* appears in an appellate court case within the District of Columbia that was decided only one month prior to the interrogation of Hinckley. In that case, *United States v. Alexander,* a suspected murderer received the following warnings, as prescribed in a D.C. police department regulation:

> You are under arrest. Before we ask any questions, you must understand what your rights are.
>
> You have the right to remain silent. You are not required to say anything to us at any time or to answer questions. Anything you say can be used against you in court.
>
> You have the right to talk to a lawyer for advice before we question you and to have him with you during questioning.
>
> If you cannot afford a lawyer and want one, a lawyer will be provided for you.
>
> If you want to answer questions now without a lawyer present you will still have the right to stop answering at any time. You also have the right to stop answering at any time until you talk to a lawyer.

Following a reading of the warnings to the suspect, she was presented with a printed waiver form, on which the first three questions were:

1. Have you read or had read to you the warnings as to your rights?

2. Do you understand these rights?

3. Do you wish to answer any questions?

Alongside each of the foregoing questions the suspect wrote "Yes." The next question was: Do you wish to answer any questions?

4. Are you willing to answer questions without having an attorney present?

To this fourth question the suspect wrote "No." The next item on the form was:

5. Signature of defendant on line below.

After the suspect's signature, the remaining portions of the waiver document contained space for the time, date, and lines for the signatures of two witnesses.

Following completion of the printed waiver form, a police officer told the suspect, "we know you are responsible for the stabbing," whereupon she confessed and agreed to give a written statement. At this point, the officer issued "fresh *Miranda* warnings."

The trial court in *Alexander* suppressed the resulting confession, for the same reason stated in the *Hinckley* case—the questioning of a custodial suspect after an indication of an interest in having a lawyer present. The suppression order was affirmed by the appellate court. Consequently, the confession could not be used as evidence at trial.

Miranda Is Being Overapplied

The warnings that were used in the *Alexander* case presumably were the same ones that were given by the D.C. police department to Hinckley. In those warnings and in the waiver forms, the police went far beyond what the Supreme Court mandated in *Miranda,* or in any of its subsequent decisions prior to (or since) the interrogations of Alexander and Hinckley. What the Court stated in *Miranda* was that before a custodial suspect could be interrogated

> he must be warned prior to any questioning that he has the right to remain silent, that anything he says can be used against him in a court of law, that he has the right to the presence of an attorney, and that if he cannot afford an attorney one will be appointed for him prior to any questioning if he so desires.

Following this specification of the *required warnings,* the Court proceeded to advise interrogators that the suspect's "opportunity to exercise these rights must be afforded to him throughout the interrogation," meaning that if he changed his mind and decided to remain silent or wanted an attorney present he should be accorded that privilege. But this was only a warning to interrogators, not something for incorporation into the required warnings to the suspects themselves. The Court also stated that after the issuance of the warnings, "the individual may knowingly and intelligently waive these rights and agree to answer questions or make a statement." Finally, the Court added the mandate that "unless and until such warnings and waiver are demonstrated by the prosecution at trial, no evidence obtained as a result of interrogation can be used against him."

The embellishments of the *Miranda* warnings and the ritualization of the written waiver, as exemplified in the foregoing *Hinckley* and *Alexander* cases, unquestionably have a tendency to dissuade many guilty suspects from submitting to police questioning.

Written Waivers

The practice of police resort to written waiver is another illustration of over-reaction to *Miranda.* The Court in *Miranda* made no mention of written waivers, and in one of its own subsequent decisions, *North Carolina v. Butler*, the Court specifically held that written waivers are not required. In that case the defendant, as a custodial suspect, orally waived his rights to silence and to have an attorney present, but refused when he was asked to sign a written waiver. The Supreme Court ruled that despite the refusal to sign the written waiver, the oral waiver was sufficient.

The message in *Butler* has not "trickled down" to some police departments, and even where it has, over-caution still prevails. Written warnings are still sought. . . .

Plastic "*Miranda* Cards"

Most police departments rely upon the oral issuance of both the warnings and the waiver questions. Their officers are supplied with printed plastic cards, on one side of which appear the warnings to be read, and on the other the waiver questions to be asked. Usually the phraseology on the cards is prepared, or at least approved, by the local prosecuting attorney. The warnings on a typical card are as follows:

1. You have the right to remain silent.
2. Anything you say can and will be used against you in a court of law.
3. You have the right to talk to a lawyer and have him present with you while you are being questioned.
4. If you cannot afford to hire a lawyer, one will be appointed to represent you before any questioning, if you wish.
5. You can decide at any time to exercise these rights and not answer any questions or make any statements.

The waiver questions sometimes are:

1. Do you understand each of these rights?

2. Having these rights in mind, do you wish to talk to us now?

Observe, again, the gratuitous inclusion of the fifth warning. As earlier stated, this is not a warning required by *Miranda*, but rather an expression the Supreme Court employed by way of an *admonition to interrogators* regarding their obligation in those instances where a person has already agreed to talk without an attorney being present. It was intended as a guideline in case situations where, during the course of the interrogation, a suspect decides to discontinue the conversation or asks for an attorney. The Court did not indicate that this admonition to interrogators should be included as one of the required warnings to suspects.

The inquiry on the waiver side of the card about "understanding the rights" and "bearing them in mind" is the result of caution deemed necessary by law enforcement agencies to avoid being faulted by the courts for obtaining waivers that were not made "knowingly and intelligently." This was the expression used by the Court in *Miranda*.

The phrase "knowingly and intelligently" prompts the writer to pose the following rhetorical questions for reader consideration. Assume that the person who is about to be interrogated actually committed the crime. He receives the warnings and is asked the waiver questions that have been described. If, after hearing that ritual, he decides to submit to an interrogation, does not that fact in itself display a lack of the intelligence necessary to make an intelligent waiver? With all such red-flag-waving by the interrogator, is it any wonder that many guilty suspects, the intelligent as well as some unintelligent ones, decide to remain silent or to ask for a lawyer? Presumably the Supreme Court only intended that the waiver must be knowingly made, but mischief has nevertheless resulted from attempts precisely to satisfy the presumed requirements for waiver. Why else would a waiver contain the words, "*having these rights in mind*, do you wish to talk to us now?"

What has just been stated about the plastic card guides for the oral issuance of the warnings, and for the asking of oral waivers, is true to an even greater degree when a printed form is used, . . . which requires name-initialing after each of the five segments of the set of warnings, to be followed by the suspect's signature, witnessed by two persons.

Suspects Are Receiving Multiple Warnings

In addition to over-reaction with regard to the language of the warnings and waivers, considerable mischief results from the frequently followed police practice of issuing "fresh" *Miranda* warnings every time an interrogation has been renewed by the original interrogator, or when a different interrogator becomes involved. This occurs even after the suspect waived his rights upon the first occasion, and even though only a short time has elapsed since the first set of warnings were given. Then, too, the interrogators usually are not content with an oral waiver; they will also present the suspect with a written one for his signature.

Sometimes the requested signature to a written waiver will not be forthcoming, as illustrated by the previously discussed case of *North Carolina v. Butler*. When this happens, police testimony that the suspect actually made an oral waiver may not be considered plausible at a confession suppression hearing, in light of the signature refusal. Also, defense counsel probably would contend that even assuming an oral waiver, the signature refusal evidences a change of mind, which, of course, would require a termination of the interrogation. A factor that should not be overlooked, however, in any evaluation of a situation of this type, is the natural reluctance of people generally to sign any document, regardless of the truthfulness of its disclosures.

As is implicit in what has already been stated, prosecuting attorneys (and other legal advisors to the police) also participate in the over-reaction process. Prosecutors are concerned, and understandably so, about trial court rejection of confessions, or appellate court reversals of convictions, because of some presumed flaw in the *Miranda* warnings or in the waiver. Even more damaging, however, are the super-cautious warnings and waiver forms that are prepared or approved for police usage. . . . Prosecutors seem to exercise as much meticulous care with the warnings and waivers as they do in the drafting of jury instructions for the presiding judge. Nothing must be left out! . . .

Miranda Must Be Limited, If Not Reversed

In Shakespeare's *Henry VI* the suggestion was made that "the first thing we do, let's kill all the lawyers." If we, as lawyers, continue to tolerate the kind of mischief created by *Miranda*, some laypersons may think Shakespeare's idea was not at all bad. The following suggestion is an effort to forestall such an unfortunate event, although, to be sure, there are more realistic reasons for offering it.

The Supreme Court, at the earliest opportunity, ought to overrule *Miranda*, or else uphold the validity of the test of confession admissibility enacted by Congress shortly after *Miranda*, as part of the 1968 "Omnibus Crime Bill." It provides that a confession "shall be admissible in evidence if it is voluntarily given." Congress submitted the following guidelines for determining whether a confession meets the test of voluntariness:

> The trial judge in determining the issue of voluntariness shall take into consideration all the circumstances surrounding the giving of the confession, including (1) the time elapsing between arrest and arraignment of the defendant making the confession, if it was made after arrest and before arraignment, (2) whether such defendant knew the nature of the offense with which he was charged or of which he was suspected at the time of making the confession, (3) whether or not such defendant was advised or knew that he

was not required to make any statement and that any such statement could be used against him, (4) whether or not such defendant had been advised prior to questioning of his right to the assistance of counsel; and (5) whether or not such defendant was without the assistance of counsel when questioned and when giving such confession.

The presence or absence of any of the above-mentioned factors to be taken into consideration by the judge need not be conclusive on the issue of voluntariness of the confession.

The state of Arizona enacted an identical provision in 1969. A test case should be sought, therefore, either within the federal system or within the state of Arizona, and brought to the Supreme Court as soon as possible. Alternatively, the Supreme Court on its own initiative might avail itself of a suitable opportunity to address the issue in a case that may already be in the process toward Supreme Court consideration. Meanwhile, the police and prosecutors should reconsider their *Miranda* practices, and the state as well as federal trial and appellate courts should moderate their apprehension over possible reversals because of shortcomings in *Miranda* formalities. This three-pronged approach to the problem would help diminish the mischief of *Miranda* until the Supreme Court eliminates it completely or modifies its principles in conformity with the foregoing Congressional enactment.

"The extent to which Miranda's *safe-guards protect suspects from pernicious interrogation practices is extremely limited."*

Miranda Has Not Ended Questionable Interrogation Practices

Welsh S. White

Welsh S. White was a professor of law at the University of Pittsburgh Law School. He was a recognized expert in the field of criminal procedure and evidence and wrote several books, including The Death Penalty in the Nineties: An Examination of the Modern System of Capital Punishment, *and numerous articles.*

In the following selection, White argues that the Miranda *ruling does not go far enough in protecting suspects from aggressive interrogation techniques.* Miranda *requires police to inform suspects of their basic rights to remain silent and have counsel present. However, according to White, once a suspect waives those rights there are few constitutional protections guiding the interrogation, and police are apt to employ coercive techniques in an attempt to evoke a confession.*

As interpreted by the post- *Miranda* Court, one of *Miranda*'s most striking limitations is its failure to impose significant restraints on police interrogation practices. *Miranda* provides virtually no restrictions on interrogation practices

Welsh S. White, "Restraining Pernicious Interrogation Practices," *Michigan Law Review*, vol. 99, March 2001, pp. 1,217–21, 1,246–47. Copyright © 2001 by *Michigan Law Review*. Reproduced by permission of the publisher and the author.

designed to induce *Miranda* waivers and on interrogation practices employed after waivers are obtained.

Miranda, of course, could have been interpreted to impose such restrictions. *Miranda* itself stated that "the fact of lengthy interrogation . . . before a statement is made is strong evidence that the accused did not validly waive his rights." This language could have been interpreted to mean that lengthy interrogations are generally impermissible. The *Miranda* decision's apparent disapproval of interrogation techniques described in various interrogation manuals, moreover, could have been interpreted to prohibit interrogators from employing those practices. And *Miranda*'s language imposing a heavy burden of waiver on the government could have been interpreted to preclude interrogators from employing interrogation practices that pressure suspects to give up their right to remain silent through pressing them to reveal information they are reluctant to disclose.

Few Rights Afforded During Interrogations

But post-*Miranda* cases have not interpreted *Miranda* in these ways. Neither the Supreme Court nor any lower court has ever indicated that the length of the interrogation, the interrogation tactics employed during the interrogation, or pressure exerted on the suspect to reveal information he is reluctant to disclose has any bearing on the validity of the suspect's *Miranda* waiver. On the contrary, once the suspect validly waives his *Miranda* rights, the due process voluntariness test provides the only restrictions on police interrogation practices.

The restrictions provided by that test are insubstantial. Over the past two decades, the Rehnquist Court has indicated that the post-*Miranda* due process test is essentially identical to the pre-*Miranda* test. As under the old test, confessions induced by force, threats of force, promises of protection from force, or by excessively lengthy continuous interrogations are involuntary. When these extreme techniques are absent, however, the voluntariness of a confession is determined on the basis of a totality of circumstances test, under which a court must assess both the interrogators' practices and the suspect's individual characteristics for the purpose of determining whether the suspect's will was overborne.

Even when it was most rigorously applied, this test imposed few limitations on interrogators. Except for the clear prohibition of extreme tactics, such as the use of force or the threat of force, the Court provided few, if any, guidelines as to what practices were prohibited. Indeed, an interrogation practice impermissible in one case might be entirely permissible in another case involving different circumstances. Interrogators operating in this environment of legal uncertainty were naturally inclined to err on the side of law enforcement interests, employing any interrogation techniques not expressly prohibited. Lower courts similarly lacked guidelines for applying the voluntariness test and struggled to determine whether particular interrogation techniques were impermissible.

Indeed, the limitations of the pre-*Miranda* voluntariness test prompted the Court to seek [in the words of Walter Schaefer] "some automatic device by which the potential evils of incommunicado interrogation [could] be controlled." Simultaneously, those concerned with restraining pernicious interrogation practices sought a constitutional rule that would impose effective, general restraints on the police. *Miranda* represented the solution to these problems. To the extent that the Court intended *Miranda* to replace the due process voluntariness test, however, the *Miranda* Court did not contemplate the important role that the due process voluntariness test would continue to play in regulating post-waiver interrogation practices.

Miranda Makes It Difficult to Prove Coercion

Ironically, *Miranda*'s practical limitations may have derived from the fact that *Miranda* effectively reduced the efficacy of the due process voluntariness test. Although the pre-*Miranda* due process test constantly shifted and evolved, the Warren Court applied the test with increasing strictness in the decade before *Miranda* was decided. *Miranda* halted this trend. In the post-*Miranda* era, the Court has equated a confession involuntary under the due process test with one that is compelled under the Fifth Amendment privilege. In *Dickerson* [*v. United States* (2000)] the Court acknowledged that, when the police have "adhered to the dictates of *Miranda*," a defendant will rarely be able to make even "a colorable argument that [his] self-incriminating statement was 'compelled.'" Lower court decisions corroborate the view expressed in *Dickerson*. A survey of recent decisions suggests that, when the police have complied with *Miranda*, it is very difficult for a defendant to establish that a confession obtained after a *Miranda* waiver violated due process.

Two factors have contributed to the infrequency with which lower courts find due process violations in post-waiver confession cases. First, lower courts conflate the test for determining a valid *Miranda* waiver with the test for determining a voluntary confession because the tests are so similar. Both tests require the court to assess the "totality of circumstances" to determine whether the suspect's action was voluntary. Although lower courts generally apply the two tests separately, some courts appear to equate a finding that a suspect's *Miranda* waiver was voluntary with a conclusion that her confession was also voluntary. A finding that the police have properly informed the suspect of his *Miranda* rights thus often has the effect of minimizing or eliminating the scrutiny applied to post-waiver interrogation practices.

Second, the Supreme Court's limited application of the voluntariness test during the post-*Miranda* era has probably increased lower courts' natural inclination to disfavor involuntary confession claims. During the thirty-year period prior to *Miranda*, the Supreme Court held confessions involuntary in at least twenty-three cases. In the thirty-four years since *Miranda*, however, it has held confessions involuntary in only two cases: *Mincey v. Arizona* (1978) and *Arizona v. Fulminante* (1991). As Professor Louis Michael Seidman has indicated, this "silence at the top" has undoubtedly led some lower courts to believe that claims of involuntary confessions need not be treated seriously.

Miranda's most significant limitation is thus its failure to identify and to prohibit (or even to promote the identification and prohibition of) pernicious interrogation practices. Is it appropriate to leave this problem to other institutions, such as legislatures or state courts? Based on the Court's interpretation [in *Colorado v. Connelly*] of both the Fifth Amendment privilege against self-incrimination and the Fourteenth Amendment due process clause, "interrogation techniques . . . offensive to a civilized system of justice" are unconstitutional. The Court thus has a constitutional obligation to address this issue. In order to fill the gap left by *Miranda* and the post-*Miranda* due process test, the Court should formulate rules restricting pernicious interrogation practices. . . .

Miranda Is Limited in Its Protection

In many ways, *Miranda* is a paradoxical decision. Among the Supreme Court's criminal procedure decisions, it has precipitated the most controversy and debate. As the *Dickerson* majority stated, moreover, the *Miranda* "warnings have become a part of our national culture." Nevertheless, as interpreted by the post-*Miranda* Court, the extent to which *Miranda*'s safeguards protect suspects from pernicious interrogation practices is extremely limited.

By requiring the police to warn suspects of their constitutional rights before subjecting them to custodial interrogation, *Miranda* does provide suspects with at least a theoretical opportunity to avoid interrogation or to halt it after it begins by invoking one of their rights. In practice, however, the vast majority of suspects waive their *Miranda* rights and submit to interrogation. Once the interrogation begins, the suspect's awareness of his rights fails to provide significant protection from pressures generated by sophisticated interrogators. Interrogators have the ability to structure the interrogation in such a way that the suspect will be deterred from successfully invoking his rights.

In addition, *Miranda* provides virtually no restrictions on the interrogation practices police are permitted to employ once the suspect waives his rights and submits to an interrogation. Indeed, *Miranda* may have had the unintended effect of reducing the extent to which the due process voluntariness test provides protection against such interrogation practices. As a result, although the Court has indicated that interrogation practices viewed as pernicious by society are prohibited, constitutional restrictions on such practices are minimal.

In order to address this problem, the Court first needs to determine what interrogation practices should be viewed as pernicious, and then to develop constitutional principles that will prohibit or restrain such practices. . . . The Court should refurbish the due process voluntariness test so as to prohibit interrogation practices that are substantially likely to produce untrustworthy statements. By taking this approach, the Court will not only fill a significant gap left by *Miranda* but also come closer to insuring that [as stated by the Court in *Culombe v. Connecticut*] "the terrible engine of the criminal law . . . not be used to overreach individuals who stand helpless against it."

| "Overturning Miranda *would provoke*
| *chaos and confusion."*

Miranda Should Be Amended

Jeffrey Rosen

*In the following selection Jeffrey Rosen describes the impact of
the* Miranda v. Arizona *decision and considers a proposal to
overrule it. He contends that* Miranda *has not had a significant
adverse impact on the ability of police to obtain confessions and
convict criminal suspects. In addition, overturning the decision
would result in widespread confusion among law enforcement
agencies and the public, who have become accustomed to the
rules outlined in the decision. Rather than overturning* Miranda,
*Rosen suggests that an alternative may be simply to amend it,
retaining the warning of a right to remain silent but allowing
interrogators more leeway in interviewing suspects without a
lawyer present. This compromise could lessen criticism of the*
Miranda *ruling by those who believe it impedes police procedures.*

Rosen writes for the New Republic *magazine, where he specializes in articles on the Supreme Court. He is an associate professor at the George Washington University School of Law, where
he teaches courses on constitutional law and criminal procedure.*

Paul Cassell, a conservative law professor from the University of Utah, asked the Supreme Court [in 2000] to overturn its most famous criminal-procedure decision, *Miranda v.
Arizona*. [Editor's note: In *Dickerson v. United States* (2000)

the Supreme Court upheld *Miranda* and ruled that Congress cannot legislatively overrule the *Miranda* rules.] But, while the campaign against *Miranda* comes from the right, the most powerful criticisms of the decision come from the left. It has long been obvious that the system *Miranda* enshrined protects the most sophisticated suspects, who need it least, and does little to stop police from using psychological pressure, lies, and trickery to elicit confessions from less sophisticated suspects. Nevertheless, the Court should decline the invitation to overturn *Miranda*. The Fifth Amendment to the Constitution doesn't protect suspects from being pressured to confess by trickery and deception, but it does protect them from being coerced to confess because of the mistaken belief that they have no right to remain silent. And, by failing to inform suspects of this right, the 1968 law that Cassell is urging on the Court instead of *Miranda* fails to meet the minimal requirements of the Constitution.

As Peter Brooks notes in his ... book, *Troubling Confessions*, ever since the Fourth Lateran Council of 1215 imposed on the faithful an annual duty to confess, confessions have triggered absolution by the church, not punishment by the state. The exception, however, was inquisitions into heretical beliefs or thought crimes. And these star-chamber investigations—in which suspects were forced to take an oath promising to answer any question that might be put to them about their most intimate thoughts and beliefs—were precisely what the Fifth Amendment was designed to prohibit. In an age that took oaths seriously, it was considered moral torture to confront a suspected heretic with the choice between self-incrimination if he confessed his private thoughts, punishment for contempt if he refused to answer, and eternal damnation if he confessed falsely and committed perjury.

Attempting to Alleviate Pressure

As a result, in America, criminal suspects in police custody are not interrogated under oath. And, although the federal government, like many states, has laws on the books forbidding lying, even while not under oath, to investigating officials, these laws are rarely enforced. Nevertheless, in light of what Chief Justice [Earl] Warren in *Miranda* called the "inherent pressures of the interrogation atmosphere," some suspects may mistakenly believe that the police will punish them if they refuse to talk—by keeping them incommunicado until they confess or by resorting to the third-degree methods that, as any fan of [the 1960s TV series] *The Untouchables* will recall, were once common.

Miranda sought to alleviate this particular pressure by requiring that all suspects be told they have the right to remain silent. It was Warren's hope that the warning would ensure that suspects who waive their right to silence make this choice, to use his words in *Miranda*, "knowingly, voluntarily, and intelligently." But, in subsequent cases, the Court abandoned this expansive interpretation of the right not to incriminate oneself. Rather than a right not to be duped into confessing, the Court came to see the Fifth Amendment as a right not to be compelled to confess. Thus, after reciting the warnings, interrogators are free to use whatever psychological pressures they please to fool suspects into waiving their rights. This can range from informing a suspect, correctly, that the court will treat him more leniently if he pleads guilty, to lying to a suspect by saying, for example, that a co-conspirator has turned against him. Either way, under *Miranda*, a suspect who confesses after being warned is presumed to have confessed voluntarily, even if he has confessed against his interest as a result of his own foolishness or the police's deception. This is why many police prefer *Miranda* to real oversight of their secret interrogations, such as videotaping.

No Hindrance to Interrogators

Miranda has not proved a major hindrance to police interrogators. Between 80 and 90 percent of all suspects waive their

Miranda rights, and more than 90 percent of all felony convictions in America result from guilty pleas, either by confession or plea bargain. In short, *Miranda* has failed to achieve its original goal—allowing suspects to protect themselves against coercive police interrogation by cutting off questioning after it has started. As William Stuntz of the University of Virginia has shown, suspects almost never stop talking once they have begun.

In fact, the practical effects of *Miranda* stem not from its first set of warnings—"You have the right to remain silent. Anything you say can and will be used against you in a court of law"—but from subsequent interpretations of its second set: "You have the right to consult with a lawyer. . . . If you cannot afford a lawyer, one will be appointed for you." In the case of *Edwards v. Arizona*, decided in 1981, the Supreme Court ruled that when a suspect says the magic words—"I want a lawyer"—interrogation must stop and cannot resume unless the suspect initiates the conversation. As a result, the first lesson that students of criminal procedure learn is that if you're suspected of a crime, whether you're innocent or guilty, you should resist the impulse to tell your side of the story and instead call [famed defense lawyer] Alan Dershowitz immediately. Sophisticated white-collar suspects—who make up a large proportion of federal criminal defendants—know this; whether or not they are read their rights, savvy suspects will demand a lawyer and say no more. But, as Stuntz argues, these suspects are not protecting themselves against police coercion; they are manipulating the system to their own advantage.

Should *Miranda* Be Overruled?

In . . . *Dickerson v. United States*, Paul Cassell . . . resurrected a law that Congress passed in 1968 to overturn *Miranda* but that has been ignored for more than three decades because

Republicans and Democrats questioned its constitutionality. In *Miranda*, Chief Justice Warren stressed that although the precise words of the *Miranda* warnings aren't constitutionally required, some form of warning is. Congress and the states are free to develop other safeguards against self-incrimination, Warren held, as long as these alternatives are "fully as effective as those described above in informing accused persons of their right of silence and in affording a continuous opportunity to exercise it." Because the alternative Congress passed in 1968 contains no requirement that suspects be notified of their right of silence, the Supreme Court can't uphold it without overruling *Miranda*.

But should *Miranda*, with all its problems, be overruled? The 1968 statute would return the law to its pre-*Miranda* state—by making the "voluntariness" of a confession the test of its admissibility. Voluntariness is to be judged by a series of amorphous factors, including whether or not the *Miranda* warnings were given. But voluntariness is a difficult standard for judges to apply, because, as courts discovered in the years leading up to *Miranda*, no one can agree on what it means to confess voluntarily. In an opinion written five years before *Miranda*, Justice Felix Frankfurter struggled to distinguish confessions "naturally born of remorse" from those produced by "an overborne will," in which "the suction process" has drained the prisoner's "capacity for freedom of choice." But Frankfurter's high standard—that confessions must be "the product of an essentially free and unconstrained choice"— proved notoriously hard to apply. Except in the rare case of a suspect who walks into the police station and confesses because he wants to expunge his guilt, confessions are always produced under circumstances designed to constrain a suspect's free choice and to induce him into acting against his best interests by speaking, instead of hiring a lawyer to speak for him.

The Case for Adhering to Precedent

As a practical matter, Frankfurter and other judges disagreed about how much pressure was undue pressure, because it was so hard to balance the relevant factors that might constrain rational choice, including the age and mental ability of the suspect, the length of the investigation, the aggressiveness of the police duplicity, and so forth. For this reason, Justice Hugo Black, at the *Miranda* oral argument, announced, "If you are going to determine the admissibility of a confession each time on the circumstances . . . if the Court will take them one by one it is more than we are capable of doing."

Miranda deftly short-circuited the legal, philosophical, and psychological debates about voluntariness, and this should weigh heavily on the swing Supreme Court justices, Sandra Day O'Connor and Anthony Kennedy, who appear uncertain about whether or not to overturn it. In *Casey v. Planned Parenthood* in 1992, O'Connor and Kennedy announced that they would uphold the core of *Roe v. Wade*, even though they may have disagreed with it when it was first decided, because Americans had come to rely on the right recognized in *Roe*, and nothing about the right had become unworkable in light of subsequent changes in society. In *Miranda*, the case for adherence to precedent is even stronger: thanks to television, there is no other right that has generated such widespread expectations. Thus, overturning *Miranda* would provoke chaos and confusion, as states struggled to adopt a host of inconsistent standards and judges struggled to apply them.

Balancing the Needs of Police and Suspects

This doesn't mean, however, that *Miranda* is the best or the only way of regulating custodial interrogation. . . . Congress and the states could consider more effective ways of balancing the needs of the police against the rights of suspects. Any constitutionally permissible alternative would have to inform suspects that they have the right to remain silent. But it might not have to include the second and more significant part of the *Miranda* warnings: informing suspects they have the right to have a lawyer present during interrogation. Indeed, as Stuntz suggests, Congress and the states might plausibly pass laws giving police the right to interrogate a suspect without a lawyer for a reasonable period of time—say, twelve hours. If a suspect asked for counsel, the interrogation wouldn't automatically cease, as it does under current law, although repeated requests for counsel might have to be respected. To regulate and deter overbearing police conduct, the entire interrogation could be videotaped.

A compromise like this might come close to satisfying *Miranda*'s critics. In his Supreme Court brief, Cassell [chose] not to emphasize his original (and hotly disputed) claim that after *Miranda*, the nationwide confession rate fell by about 16 percentage points; now Cassell argues that even if *Miranda* were overturned, the police would and should continue giving *Miranda* warnings anyway, just to be safe. The real benefit of overturning *Miranda*, Cassell claims, would be to allow police more leeway to question suspects without lawyers. But Congress and the states may have this power anyway, even if the Supreme Court reaffirms the core of *Miranda*.

A system in which police could question suspects without lawyers would, of course, bring us even further from the ideal that Warren embraced—namely, that the decision to confess should be made "voluntarily, knowingly, and intelligently." The only way of achieving that ideal would be to put a Dershowitz in every interrogation room. But as long as our legal system, like our culture, continues to rely on public confessions, perhaps we should inform suspects of their right to silence in a way that gives police more discretion, not less, in pressuring suspects to act against their own best interests. After all, as [University of Virginia law professor] Peter Brooks notes, "It may be that the only true confessions are involuntary."

CHAPTER 3

Defining the Right
to Privacy

Case Overview

Katz v. United States (1967)

The Supreme Court case of *Katz v. United States* expanded the concept of privacy. In previous cases the Court had ruled that a warrant was necessary to search a person's home or belongings. In *Katz* the Court ruled that a suspect's conversations were also protected against warrantless intrusions—even if the conversations took place in public—as long as the person had "a reasonable expectation of privacy." In such a situation those conversations could not be recorded and used against the suspect in court.

The case that led to this new interpretation was that of Charles Katz, a Los Angeles bookie who was using a public pay phone to place wagers. The FBI placed a wiretap on the phone, without a warrant, and recorded Katz placing bets in Florida and Boston. He was arrested and convicted of illegal gambling.

Katz appealed the decision, based on his Fourth Amendment right to privacy. The California court of appeals upheld the conviction. It claimed that because the FBI did not physically intrude upon the phone booth, no warrant was required for the surveillance. Moreover, because the phone booth was in a public location, Katz did not have a right to privacy. The case was brought before the Supreme Court in October 1967.

The Supreme Court overturned that ruling in a 7-1 decision. The Court held that personal privacy is not limited to place. This declaration overturned a previous ruling in *Olmstead v. United States* (1928), which had stated that the application of the Fourth Amendment was limited to physical objects and places. Instead, the Court in *Katz* stated that "the Fourth Amendment protects people, not places." Therefore, a person has a right to privacy even in public. The Court also established the concept of a reasonable expectation of privacy. This meant that if an objective observer would consider that a person had a right to expect privacy, then the situation should be covered by the Fourth Amendment. Since Katz had essentially rented the telephone booth by paying for his call, the Court concluded he had a reasonable expectation that his conversation would be private.

Katz v. United States has had a broad reach as constantly changing technology has forced the courts to deal with new challenges to privacy and law enforcement. In his dissent, Justice Hugo Black stated that the original framers of the Constitution could not have envisioned a telephone and thus did not explicitly mention it. So, too, those who decided this case could not have envisioned the various telecommunication and information-gathering devices that would follow. However, the ruling has provided a framework for cases dealing with such devices.

> "What a person ... seeks to preserve as private, even in an area accessible to the public, may be constitutionally protected."

The Court's Decision: The Fourth Amendment Protects Private Communications

Potter Stewart

The case of Katz v. United States *redefined the concept of personal privacy. Charles Katz was arrested for interstate gambling after the FBI placed a recording device on the phone booth he used to make wagers. Though the FBI did not have a warrant, the lower courts ruled that since Katz was in a public place, he did not have an expectation of privacy. Therefore the wiretapping did not violate his Fourth Amendment right to be free from unreasonable searches and seizures.*

In Katz v. United States *the Supreme Court rejected this conclusion. In the majority opinion, excerpted here, Potter Stewart explains that personal privacy guaranteed by the Fourth Amendment is not limited to a place such as a home or office. It is relevant wherever a person has a reasonable expectation of privacy, including a public telephone booth. Therefore, a warrant must be issued before the personal communications of a person in a public place can be intercepted by means of wiretapping or other forms of surveillance.*

Potter Stewart was appointed to the Supreme Court in 1958 and served until his retirement in 1981. He was known as a moderate on the Court.

Potter Stewart, majority opinion, *Katz v. United States*, December 18, 1967.

The petitioner was convicted in the District Court for the
Southern District of California under an eight-count indictment charging him with transmitting wagering information by telephone from Los Angeles to Miami and Boston, in
violation of a federal statute. At trial the Government was permitted, over the petitioner's objection, to introduce evidence
of the petitioner's end of telephone conversations, overheard
by FBI agents who had attached an electronic listening and recording device to the outside of the public telephone booth
from which he had placed his calls. In affirming his conviction, the Court of Appeals rejected the contention that the recordings had been obtained in violation of the Fourth Amendment, because "there was no physical entrance into the area
occupied by [the petitioner]." We granted certiorari [that is,
the Court agreed to hear the case] in order to consider the
constitutional questions thus presented.

The petitioner has phrased those questions as follows:

A. Whether a public telephone booth is a constitutionally
protected area so that evidence obtained by attaching an
electronic listening recording device to the top of such a
booth is obtained in violation of the right to privacy of the
user of the booth.

B. Whether physical penetration of a constitutionally protected area is necessary before a search and seizure can be
said to be violative of the Fourth Amendment to the United
States Constitution.

We decline to adopt this formulation of the issues. In the first
place, the correct solution of Fourth Amendment problems is
not necessarily promoted by incantation of the phrase "constitutionally protected area." Secondly, the Fourth Amendment
cannot be translated into a general constitutional "right to
privacy." That Amendment protects individual privacy against
certain kinds of governmental intrusion, but its protections go
further, and often have nothing to do with privacy at all.

Other provisions of the Constitution protect personal privacy from other forms of governmental invasion. But the protection of a person's general right to privacy—his right to be let alone by other people—is, like the protection of his property and of his very life, left largely to the law of the individual States.

Personal Privacy Is Not Limited to Place

Because of the misleading way the issues have been formulated, the parties have attached great significance to the characterization of the telephone booth from which the petitioner placed his calls. The petitioner has strenuously argued that the booth was a "constitutionally protected area." The Government has maintained with equal vigor that it was not. But this effort to decide whether or not a given "area," viewed in the abstract, is "constitutionally protected" deflects attention from the problem presented by this case. For the Fourth Amendment protects people, not places. What a person knowingly exposes to the public, even in his own home or office, is not a subject of Fourth Amendment protection. But what he seeks to preserve as private, even in an area accessible to the public, may be constitutionally protected.

The Government stresses the fact that the telephone booth from which the petitioner made his calls was constructed partly of glass, so that he was as visible after he entered it as he would have been if he had remained outside. But what he sought to exclude when he entered the booth was not the intruding eye—it was the uninvited ear. He did not shed his right to do so simply because he made his calls from a place where he might be seen. No less than an individual in a business office, in a friend's apartment, or in a taxicab, a person in a telephone booth may rely upon the protection of the Fourth Amendment. One who occupies it, shuts the door behind him, and pays the toll that permits him to place a call is surely entitled to assume that the words he utters into the mouthpiece will not be broadcast to the world. To read the Constitution more narrowly is to ignore the vital role that the public telephone has come to play in private communication.

A Broader View of Fourth Amendment Protection

The Government contends, however, that the activities of its agents in this case should not be tested by Fourth Amendment requirements, for the surveillance technique they employed involved no physical penetration of the telephone booth from which the petitioner placed his calls. It is true that the absence of such penetration was at one time thought to foreclose further Fourth Amendment inquiry, for that Amendment was thought to limit only searches and seizures of tangible property. But "the premise that property interests control the right of the Government to search and seize has been discredited." *Warden v. Hayden.* Thus, although a closely divided Court supposed in *Olmstead [v. United States]* that surveillance without any trespass and without the seizure of any material object fell outside the ambit of the Constitution, we have since departed from the narrow view on which that decision rested. Indeed, we have expressly held that the Fourth Amendment governs not only the seizure of tangible items, but extends as well to the recording of oral statements, overheard without any "technical trespass under . . . local property law." *Silverman v. United States.* Once this much is acknowledged, and once it is recognized that the Fourth Amendment protects people—and not simply "areas"—against unreasonable searches and seizures, it becomes clear that the reach of that Amendment cannot turn upon the presence or absence of a physical intrusion into any given enclosure.

We conclude that the underpinnings of *Olmstead* and *Goldman [v. United States]* have been so eroded by our subsequent decisions that the "trespass" doctrine there enunciated can no longer be regarded as controlling. The Government's activities in electronically listening to and recording the petitioner's words violated the privacy upon which he justifiably relied while using the telephone booth and thus constituted a "search and seizure" within the meaning of the Fourth Amendment. The fact that the electronic device employed to achieve that end did not happen to penetrate the wall of the booth can have no constitutional significance.

The question remaining for decision, then, is whether the search and seizure conducted in this case complied with constitutional standards. In that regard, the Government's position is that its agents acted in an entirely defensible manner: They did not begin their electronic surveillance until investigation of the petitioner's activities had established a strong probability that he was using the telephone in question to transmit gambling information to persons in other States, in violation of federal law. Moreover, the surveillance was limited, both in scope and in duration, to the specific purpose of establishing the contents of the petitioner's unlawful telephonic communications. The agents confined their surveillance to the brief periods during which he used the telephone booth, and they took great care to overhear only the conversations of the petitioner himself.

Even in Public Places, a Warrant Is Necessary

Accepting this account of the Government's actions as accurate, it is clear that this surveillance was so narrowly circumscribed that a duly authorized magistrate, properly notified of the need for such investigation, specifically informed of the basis on which it was to proceed, and clearly apprised of the precise intrusion it would entail, could constitutionally have authorized, with appropriate safeguards, the very limited search and seizure that the Government asserts in fact took place. Only last Term we sustained the validity of such an authorization, holding that, under sufficiently "precise and discriminate circumstances," a federal court may empower government agents to employ a concealed electronic device "for the narrow and particularized purpose of ascertaining the truth of the . . . allegations" of a "detailed factual affidavit alleging the commission of a specific criminal offense." *Osborn v. United States.* Discussing that holding, the Court in *Berger v. New York,* said that "the order authorizing the use of the electronic device" in *Osborn* "afforded similar protections to those . . . of conventional warrants authorizing the seizure of tangible evidence." Through those protections, "no greater invasion of privacy was permitted than was necessary under the circumstances." Here, too, a similar judicial order could have accommodated "the legitimate needs of law enforcement" by authorizing the carefully limited use of electronic surveillance.

The Government urges that, because its agents relied upon the decisions in *Olmstead* and *Goldman,* and because they did no more here than they might properly have done with prior judicial sanction, we should retroactively validate their conduct. That we cannot do. It is apparent that the agents in this case acted with restraint. Yet the inescapable fact is that this restraint was imposed by the agents themselves, not by a judicial officer. They were not required, before commencing the search, to present their estimate of probable cause for detached scrutiny by a neutral magistrate. They were not compelled, during the conduct of the search itself, to observe precise limits established in advance by a specific court order. Nor were they directed, after the search had been completed, to notify the authorizing magistrate in detail of all that had been seized. In the absence of such safeguards, this Court has never sustained a search upon the sole ground that officers reasonably expected to find evidence of a particular crime and voluntarily confined their activities to the least intrusive means consistent with that end. Searches conducted without warrants have been held unlawful "notwithstanding facts unquestionably showing probable cause," [*Agnello v. United States*] for the

Constitution requires "that the deliberate, impartial judgment of a judicial officer . . . be interposed between the citizen and the police. . . ." *Wong Sun v. United States.* "Over and again this Court has emphasized that the mandate of the [Fourth] Amendment requires adherence to judicial processes," [*United States v. Jeffers*] and that searches conducted outside the judicial process, without prior approval by judge or magistrate, are per se unreasonable under the Fourth Amendment—subject only to a few specifically established and well-delineated exceptions.

No Exception to Requirement of a Warrant

It is difficult to imagine how any of those exceptions could ever apply to the sort of search and seizure involved in this case. Even electronic surveillance substantially contemporaneous with an individual's arrest could hardly be deemed an "incident" of that arrest. Nor could the use of electronic surveillance without prior authorization be justified on grounds of "hot pursuit." And, of course, the very nature of electronic surveillance precludes its use pursuant to the suspect's consent.

The Government does not question these basic principles. Rather, it urges the creation of a new exception to cover this case. It argues that surveillance of a telephone booth should be exempted from the usual requirement of advance authorization by a magistrate upon a showing of probable cause. We cannot agree. Omission of such authorization

> bypasses the safeguards provided by an objective predetermination of probable cause, and substitutes instead the far less reliable procedure of an after-the-event justification for the . . . search, too likely to be subtly influenced by the familiar shortcomings of hindsight judgment. *Beck v. Ohio.*

And bypassing a neutral predetermination of the scope of a search leaves individuals secure from Fourth Amendment violations "only in the discretion of the police." [*Beck v. Ohio*].

These considerations do not vanish when the search in question is transferred from the setting of a home, an office, or a hotel room to that of a telephone booth. Wherever a man may be, he is entitled to know that he will remain free from unreasonable searches and seizures. The government agents here ignored "the procedure of antecedent justification . . . that is central to the Fourth Amendment" [*Osborne v. United States*], a procedure that we hold to be a constitutional precondition of the kind of electronic surveillance involved in this case. Because the surveillance here failed to meet that condition, and because it led to the petitioner's conviction, the judgment must be reversed.

"No general right is created by the [Fourth] Amendment so as to give this Court the unlimited power to hold unconstitutional everything which affects privacy."

Dissenting Opinion: The Fourth Amendment Does Not Protect a Broad Right to Privacy

Hugo L. Black

In the case of Katz v. United States, *the Supreme Court ruled that FBI officers had violated a suspect's Fourth Amendment rights against unreasonable searches and seizures by recording his conversation in a public phone booth. Black disagreed with this ruling and wrote the following dissent.*

Black holds that a wiretap does not constitute a search or seizure and therefore does not violate the Fourth Amendment. He notes that in all previous cases the Court has interpreted the Fourth Amendment as regulating searches and seizures of tangible items. Overhearing a conversation, either by standing next to someone or by tapping a phone, is not equivalent to searching a suspect's home or seizing his or her papers. Black objects to what he sees as the Court's movement to read into the Fourth Amendment a broad right to privacy, which he believes exceeds the intentions of the framers of the Constitution.

Black served on the Supreme Court from 1937 to his retirement in 1971. He was a controversial appointee due to his

Hugo L. Black, dissenting opinion, *Katz v. United States*, December 18, 1967.

prior membership in the Ku Klux Klan in the early 1920s. He denounced the Klan shortly after joining and went on to support the civil rights movement.

If I could agree with the Court that eavesdropping carried on by electronic means (equivalent to wiretapping) constitutes a "search" or "seizure," I would be happy to join the Court's opinion. For on that premise my Brother [Justice Potter] Stewart sets out methods in accord with the Fourth Amendment to guide States in the enactment and enforcement of laws passed to regulate wiretapping by government. In this respect today's opinion differs sharply from *Berger v. New York*, decided last Term, which held void on its face a New York statute authorizing wiretapping on warrants issued by magistrates on showings of probable cause. The *Berger* case also set up what appeared to be insuperable obstacles to the valid passage of such wiretapping laws by States. The Court's opinion in this case, however, removes the doubts about state power in this field and abates to a large extent the confusion and near-paralyzing effect of the *Berger* holding. Notwithstanding these good efforts of the Court, I am still unable to agree with its interpretation of the Fourth Amendment.

My basic objection is twofold: (1) I do not believe that the words of the Amendment will bear the meaning given them by today's decision, and (2) I do not believe that it is the proper role of this Court to rewrite the Amendment in order "to bring it into harmony with the times" and thus reach a result that many people believe to be desirable.

The Fourth Amendment Only Covers Tangible Items

While I realize that an argument based on the meaning of words lacks the scope, and no doubt the appeal, of broad policy discussions and philosophical discourses on such nebulous subjects as privacy, for me the language of the Amendment is the crucial place to look in construing a written document such as our Constitution. The Fourth Amendment says that

> The right of the people to be secure in their persons, houses, papers, and effects, against unreasonable searches and seizures, shall not be violated, and no Warrants shall issue, but upon probable cause, supported by Oath or affirmation, and particularly describing the place to be searched, and the persons or things to be seized.

The first clause protects "persons, houses, papers, and effects, against unreasonable searches and seizures...." These words connote the idea of tangible things with size, form, and weight, things capable of being searched, seized, or both. The second clause of the Amendment still further establishes its Framers' purpose to limit its protection to tangible things by providing that no warrants shall issue but those "particularly describing the place to be searched, and the persons or things to be seized." A conversation overheard by eavesdropping, whether by plain snooping or wiretapping, is not tangible and, under the normally accepted meanings of the words, can neither be searched nor seized. In addition the language of the second clause indicates that the Amendment refers not only to something tangible so it can be seized but to something already in existence so it can be described. Yet the Court's interpretation would have the Amendment apply to overhearing future conversations which by their very nature are nonexistent until they take place. How can one "describe" a future conversation, and, if one cannot, how can a magistrate issue a warrant to eavesdrop one in the future? It is argued that information showing what is expected to be said is sufficient to limit the boundaries of what later can be admitted into evidence; but does such general information really meet the specific language of the Amendment which says "particularly describing"? Rather than using language in a completely artificial way, I must conclude that the Fourth Amendment simply does not apply to eavesdropping.

The Fourth Amendment Does Not Prohibit Eavesdropping

Tapping telephone wires, of course, was an unknown possibility at the time the Fourth Amendment was adopted. But eavesdropping (and wiretapping is nothing more than eavesdropping by telephone) was, as even the majority opinion in *Berger* recognized, "an ancient practice which at common law was condemned as a nuisance. In those days the eavesdropper listened by naked ear under the eaves of houses or their windows, or beyond their walls seeking out private discourse." There can be no doubt that the Framers were aware of this practice, and if they had desired to outlaw or restrict the use of evidence obtained by eavesdropping, I believe that they would have used the appropriate language to do so in the Fourth Amendment. They certainly would not have left such a task to the ingenuity of language-stretching judges. No one, it seems to me, can read the debates on the Bill of Rights without reaching the conclusion that its Framers and critics well knew the meaning of the words they used, what they would be understood to mean by others, their scope and their limitations. Under these circumstances it strikes me as a charge against their scholarship, their common sense and their candor to give to the Fourth Amendment's language the eavesdropping meaning the Court imputes to it today.

I do not deny that common sense requires and that this Court often has said that the Bill of Rights' safeguards should be given a liberal construction. This principle, however, does not justify construing the search and seizure amendment as applying to eavesdropping or the "seizure" of conversations. The Fourth Amendment was aimed directly at the abhorred practice of breaking in, ransacking and searching homes and other buildings and seizing people's personal belongings without warrants issued by magistrates. The Amendment deserves, and this Court has given it, a liberal construction in order to protect against warrantless searches of buildings and seizures of tangible personal effects. But until today this Court has refused to say that eavesdropping comes within the ambit of Fourth Amendment restrictions.

Prior Cases Have Held That Conversations Are Not Covered

So far I have attempted to state why I think the words of the Fourth Amendment prevent its application to eavesdropping. It is important now to show that this has been the traditional view of the Amendment's scope since its adoption and that the Court's decision in this case, along with its amorphous holding in *Berger* last Term, marks the first real departure from that view.

The first case to reach this Court which actually involved a clear-cut test of the Fourth Amendment's applicability to eavesdropping through a wiretap was, of course, *Olmstead* [*v. United States*]. In holding that the interception of private telephone conversations by means of wiretapping was not a violation of the Fourth Amendment, this Court, speaking through Mr. Chief Justice [William Howard] Taft, examined the language of the Amendment and found, just as I do now, that the words could not be stretched to encompass overheard conversations. . . .

Goldman v. United States is an even clearer example of this Court's traditional refusal to consider eavesdropping as being covered by the Fourth Amendment. There federal agents used a detectaphone, which was placed on the wall of an adjoining room, to listen to the conversation of a defendant carried on in his private office and intended to be confined within the four walls of the room. This Court, referring to *Olmstead*, found no Fourth Amendment violation.

No Fourth Amendment Violation

It should be noted that the Court in *Olmstead* based its decision squarely on the fact that wiretapping or eavesdropping does not violate the Fourth Amendment. As shown in the cited quotation from the case, the Court went to great pains to examine the actual language of the Amendment and found that the words used simply could not be stretched to cover eavesdropping. That there was no trespass was not the determinative factor, and indeed the Court in citing *Hester v. United States*, indicated that even where there was a trespass the Fourth Amendment does not automatically apply to evidence obtained by "hearing or sight." The *Olmstead* majority characterized *Hester* as holding "that the testimony of two officers of the law who trespassed on the defendant's land, concealed themselves one hundred yards away from his house and saw him come out and hand a bottle of whiskey to another, was not inadmissible. While there was a trespass, there was no search of person, house, papers or effects." Thus the clear holding of the *Olmstead* and *Goldman* cases, undiluted by any question of trespass, is that eavesdropping, in both its original and modern forms, is not violative of the Fourth Amendment. . . .

Silverman Did Not Change Precedent

To support its new interpretation of the Fourth Amendment, which in effect amounts to a rewriting of the language, the Court's opinion concludes that "the underpinnings of *Olmstead* and *Goldman* have been . . . eroded by our subsequent decisions. . . ." But the only cases cited as accomplishing this "eroding" are *Silverman v. United States* and *Warden v. Hayden*. Neither of these cases "eroded" *Olmstead* or *Goldman*. *Silverman* is an interesting choice since there the Court expressly refused to re-examine the rationale of *Olmstead* or *Goldman* although such a re-examination was strenuously urged upon the Court by the petitioners' counsel. Also it is significant that in *Silverman*, as the Court described it, "the eavesdropping was accomplished by means of an unauthorized physical penetration into the premises occupied by the petitioners," thus calling into play the supervisory exclusionary rule of evidence. As I have pointed out above, where there is an unauthorized intrusion, this Court has rejected admission of evidence obtained regardless of whether there has been an unconstitutional search and seizure. The majority's decision here relies heavily on the statement in the opinion that the Court "need not pause to consider whether or not there was a technical trespass under the local property law relating to party walls." Yet this statement should not becloud the fact that time and again the opinion emphasizes that there has been an unauthorized intrusion. . . . In light of this and the fact that the Court expressly refused to re-examine *Olmstead* and *Goldman*, I cannot read *Silverman* as overturning the interpretation stated very plainly in *Olmstead* and followed in *Goldman* that eavesdropping is not covered by the Fourth Amendment.

Olmstead and *Goldman* Remain Good Law

The other "eroding" case cited in the Court's opinion is *Warden v. Hayden*. It appears that this case is cited for the proposition that the Fourth Amendment applies to "intangibles," such as conversation, and the following ambiguous statement is quoted from the opinion: "The premise that property interests control the right of the Government to search and seize has been discredited." But far from being concerned with eavesdropping, *Warden v. Hayden* upholds the seizure of clothes, certainly tangibles by any definition. The discussion of property interests was involved only with the common-law rule that the right to seize property depended upon proof of a superior property interest.

Thus, I think that although the Court attempts to convey the impression that for some reason today *Olmstead* and *Goldman* are no longer good law, it must face up to the fact that these cases have never been overruled or even "eroded." It is the Court's opinions in this case and *Berger* which for the first time since 1791, when the Fourth Amendment was adopted, have declared that eavesdropping is subject to Fourth Amendment restrictions and that conversations can be "seized." I must align myself with all those judges who up to this year have never been able to impute such a meaning to the words of the Amendment.

The Court Misinterprets the Fourth Amendment

Since I see no way in which the words of the Fourth Amendment can be construed to apply to eavesdropping, that closes the matter for me. In interpreting the Bill of Rights, I willingly go as far as a liberal construction of the language takes me, but I simply cannot in good conscience give a meaning to words which they have never before been thought to have and which they certainly do not have in common ordinary usage. I will not distort the words of the Amendment in order to "keep the Constitution up to date" or "to bring it into harmony with the times." It was never meant that this Court have such power, which in effect would make us a continuously functioning constitutional convention.

With this decision the Court has completed, I hope, its re-writing of the Fourth Amendment, which started only recently when the Court began referring incessantly to the Fourth Amendment not so much as a law against unreasonable searches and seizures as one to protect an individual's privacy. By clever word juggling the Court finds it plausible to argue that language aimed specifically at searches and seizures of things that can be searched and seized may, to protect privacy, be applied to eavesdropped evidence of conversations that can neither be searched nor seized. Few things happen to an individual that do not affect his privacy in one way or another. Thus, by arbitrarily substituting the Court's language, designed to protect privacy, for the Constitution's language, designed to protect against unreasonable searches and seizures, the Court has made the Fourth Amendment its vehicle for holding all laws violative of the Constitution which offend the Court's broadest concept of privacy. As I said in *Griswold v. Connecticut*, "The Court talks about a constitutional 'right of privacy' as though there is some constitutional provision or provisions forbidding any law ever to be passed which might abridge the 'privacy' of individuals. But there is not." I made clear in that dissent my fear of the dangers involved when this Court uses the "broad, abstract and ambiguous concept" of "privacy" as a "comprehensive substitute for the Fourth Amendment's guarantee against 'unreasonable searches and seizures.'"

The Fourth Amendment protects privacy only to the extent that it prohibits unreasonable searches and seizures of "persons, houses, papers, and effects." No general right is created by the Amendment so as to give this Court the unlimited power to hold unconstitutional everything which affects privacy. Certainly the Framers, well acquainted as they were with the excesses of governmental power, did not intend to grant this Court such omnipotent lawmaking authority as that. The history of governments proves that it is dangerous to freedom to repose such powers in courts.

*"The 'reasonable expectation of privacy'
test which* Katz v. United States *gave
us to determine at what point the
Fourth Amendment's protections attach
is here to stay."*

Katz Affords Protection Against High-Tech Privacy Intrusions

Richard S. Julie

The Supreme Court's decision in Katz v. United States *was a response to new surveillance technologies that made it easier for investigators to intrude on people's privacy and observe their actions and words. A majority of justices believed these developments required a rethinking of the right to privacy afforded by the Fourth Amendment. The Court ruled that the right applied to people, including their telephone conversations, and not just places, such as homes and offices. Since that time technological changes have resulted in even more intrusive technologies for surveillance, including devices that can gather information from within a dwelling without ever entering it and cameras that can take accurate pictures of individuals from satellites.*

In the following selection Richard S. Julie summarizes the Court's decision in Katz *and describes the new standard it set for determining in what situation a person has a "reasonable expectation of privacy" deserving of Fourth Amendment protection.*

Richard S. Julie, "High-Tech Surveillance Tools and the Fourth Amendment: Reasonable Expectations of Privacy in the Technological Age," *American Criminal Law Review*, vol. 37, no. 1, Winter 2000, pp. 127–43. Copyright © 2000 by *American Criminal Law Review*. Reproduced by permission.

He contends that the broader definition of privacy established in Katz *was necessary in light of increasingly invasive technologies.*

Julie is an associate attorney at the law firm of Young Conaway Stargatt & Taylor in Delaware. He has written several articles on criminal procedure and law enforcement.

In the absence of a search (or seizure), the Fourth Amendment is not implicated by police action. For nearly fifty years, beginning in 1928 with *Olmstead v. United States*, the Supreme Court of the United States premised the existence of a search on whether a physical trespass had occurred under local property law. In *Katz v. United States*, largely in response to technological advances in police surveillance techniques, the Supreme Court promulgated a new standard for determining when a search has occurred, bringing Fourth Amendment jurisprudence into the twentieth century by basing the analysis on privacy interests.

Property-Based Literalism and the Fourth Amendment

The property-based conception of Fourth Amendment rights embodied in *Olmstead* entailed many flaws; this became obvious as police surveillance technology continued to advance during the forty years the decision was in effect. Adhering firmly to the precise language of the Amendment, the Court in *Olmstead* held that the only interests protected by the Fourth Amendment were those in tangible objects, such as papers, houses, and other physical possessions, and that those possessions were protected only against physical invasions. Overheard conversations and other types of communicative evidence, therefore, had no specific protection, unless obtained in violation of local property law.

The *Olmstead* decision thus embodies what Professor [Morgan] Cloud calls "property-based literalism," the theory that no search occurs where there is no physical trespass into a "constitutionally protected area" such as the home or office. The primary criticism of this approach is that it required courts to base their decisions on what would seem to be insignificant, even irrelevant, distinctions. Compare, for example, *Goldman v. United States* in which police officers' eavesdropping was held not to be a search because their microphone had been placed against a wall on the side opposite the defendant's office, with *Silverman v. United States*, in which a constitutional violation was found where police used a foot-long "spike-mike" to penetrate a party wall, entering (trespassing on) the private property of the defendant.

Katz v. United States: A Modern Approach

Olmstead's trespass-based theory of Fourth Amendment jurisprudence was ultimately rejected by the Supreme Court in *Katz v. United States*. Charles Katz was a "prolific basketball handicapper" suspected by the Federal Bureau of Investigation of illegally transmitting wagering information across state lines. Without obtaining a warrant, FBI agents attached "an electronic listening and recording device" to the outside of the public phone booth from which Katz was known to place such calls, and recorded the illegal conversations which ensued. While both Katz and the federal government phrased their arguments to the Supreme Court in terms of "constitutionally protected areas," the phraseology prescribed in *Olmstead*, the Court "declined to adopt [that] formulation of the issues." Proclaiming that "the Fourth Amendment protects people, not places," Justice [Potter] Stewart, for the Court, wrote:

> What a person knowingly exposes to the public, even in his own home or office, is not a subject of Fourth Amendment protection. But what he seeks to preserve as private, even in an area accessible to the public, may be constitutionally protected. . . . One who occupies [a phone booth], shuts the door behind him, and pays the toll that permits him to

place a call is surely entitled to assume that the words he utters into the mouthpiece will not be broadcast to the world. To read the Constitution more narrowly is to ignore the vital role that the public telephone has come to play in private communication.

The rule that *Katz* eventually came to stand for, however, is Justice [John Marshall] Harlan's "reasonable expectation of privacy" standard, embodied in the two-prong test of his concurring opinion.

A search is deemed to have occurred when (1) the government conduct has transgressed a citizen's subjective manifestation of a privacy interest: and (2) the privacy interest invaded is one that society is prepared to accept as legitimate. This "reasonable expectation of privacy" test has come to be the means used for determining the scope of the Fourth Amendment's protections.

A New Construction of Privacy

This ruling constituted a long overdue recognition that *Olmstead*'s strict interpretation of the plain language of the Fourth Amendment was insufficient, in light of continuing advances in police surveillance technology, to protect those interests which the Framers had sought to protect. The Fourth Amendment was adopted in response to the use of general warrants and writs of assistance, by which British soldiers conducted wide-scale searches of colonists' homes and private affairs for contraband. The Framers sought to curtail these abuses by establishing a minimum threshold for police intrusion into citizens' privacy. But *Olmstead*, by limiting the Amendment's scope to property law, confounded these aims. Justice [Louis] Brandeis, in stinging dissent from the *Olmstead* majority, reasoned that, because it was a constitution that the Court was expounding, which was to be applied to police tactics and equipment which did not exist at the time the Constitution was drafted, the Court had to "adopt a construction susceptible of meeting modern conditions."

The "reasonable expectation of privacy" test embodied in *Katz* is just such a construction; it recognizes that individuals have a panoply of rights, beyond those afforded by private property, which the Fourth Amendment was designed to protect. Indeed, the Court's Fourth Amendment jurisprudence in the years following *Katz* gave a broad reading to the right to privacy, indicating that the Fourth Amendment had become a vigorous source of protection for individual interests. In *Delaware v. Prouse*, for example, the Court recognized an increased expectation of privacy for automobile passengers, observing that people "find a greater sense of security and privacy in traveling in an automobile than they do in exposing themselves by pedestrian or other modes of travel."

Critiques of *Katz* and Its Progeny

Unfortunately, as members of the [chief justice Earl] Warren Court retired and were replaced by more conservative appointees, the broad reading given this privacy analysis began to be turned on its head. In recent years, the Court has tended to find that [in the words of Professor Thomas K. Clancy] "the effect of modern life, with its technological and other advances, serves to eliminate or reduce a person's justified expectation of privacy." For example, in *Dow Chemical Co. v. United States* the Court found no violation of the Fourth Amendment where the Environmental Protection Agency [EPA] engaged in warrantless aerial photographing of Dow Chemical's Michigan manufacturing plant. Dow had maintained elaborate ground security, which barred public view of its plant from the ground, and had investigated any noncommercial flights (including the EPA's) which flew low over its property and which Dow felt could compromise its trade secrets. Despite these attempts at secrecy, which would seem to evidence a subjective expectation of privacy, the Court found that because any person with access to a camera and an airplane could have taken the same photographs, it was unreasonable, under the second prong of Justice Harlan's test, for Dow to expect that its plant would remain private.

In addition to finding that new technologies reduce expectations of privacy, the Court has also tended to limit the reach of the Fourth Amendment through what Professor Clancy calls an "empirical approach," which examines whether an act is observable by the general public and concludes, if so, that it is unreasonable to expect privacy in that act. As a result, government regulation has been found to reduce (if not eliminate altogether) an individual's expectation of privacy. In *New York v. Burger,* for example, the Court held that an automotive junk dealer, who is required by statute to keep a record for police inspection of all automobiles and parts in his possession, has a reduced expectation of privacy in his business. He therefore had no constitutional objection to a warrantless (or suspicionless) search of his junkyard. The Court found, in effect, that the government may diminish through legislation the scope of protection afforded by the Constitution, eliminating various expectations of privacy at will. This would seem to violate the core principle of constitutional law, that the legislature may not alter the Constitution by an ordinary statute. As Justice Stewart explained, "the mandates of the Fourth Amendment demand heightened, not lowered, respect, as the intrusive regulatory authority of government expands."

Another common criticism of *Katz's* reasonable expectation of privacy test is that it is circular; as the argument goes, the Supreme Court protects only those expectations that are reasonable, while the only expectations that are reasonable are those which the Supreme Court is willing to protect. The Court has also been criticized because the first prong of Justice Harlan's test, that involving the subjective manifestation of the expectation of privacy, has gone largely ignored; indeed, it is not practicable if one is to base constitutional criminal procedure on the type of bright-line rules necessary for effective police work. For example, the rule of *Katz*, that there is a reasonable expectation of privacy in telephone calls made from a public phone booth, is unequivocal. Even if a particular citizen subjectively expects that the police are monitoring his calls, the Fourth Amendment prohibits the police from doing so without a warrant. Just as ignorance of the law is no defense to a criminal charge, ignorance of one's right to privacy does not effect a waiver thereof. In practice, the first prong of Justice Harlan's test is only used by courts in situations where a reasonable expectation of privacy is found not to exist. . . .

The Fourth Amendment Protects People *and* Places

The "reasonable expectation of privacy" standard promulgated in *Katz v. United States*, when viewed along with the decisions interpreting that standard, can be a robust protector of the rights of average citizens, preventing the government from, among other things, using high-tech surveillance devices to peer through their walls in the absence of judicial intervention in the form of a warrant. While *Katz* is not without its flaws, those flaws are not so critical as to warrant an overhaul in Fourth Amendment jurisprudence as substantial as the one effected by the transition from *Olmstead* to the privacy analysis. Working within the framework of *Katz*, it is possible to formulate a conception of the Fourth Amendment that will permit the government to enforce the law effectively while protecting Constitutional rights and taking account of advances in the technology which law-enforcement authorities utilize. . . .

The Supreme Court, in overruling *Olmstead*, need not have, and should not have, overruled it entirely. That part of the *Olmstead* decision that held that a search occurred only when there was a physical trespass, of course, could not stand; as Justice Brandeis wrote, "the Court had to adopt a construction susceptible of meeting modern conditions." But *Katz*'s recognition that the Fourth Amendment provides protection for intangible interests need not have been bundled with an assertion by the Court that the Fourth Amendment provides no protection for private property as such. Rather than saying that "the Fourth Amendment protects people, not places," the Court should have held that it protects both people and places.

It is possible for willing courts to extend protection to both people and places. The first prong of the *Katz* test requires that a citizen have subjectively manifested an expectation of privacy. It is arguable that citizens of the several states subjectively expect that others will abide by their states' laws governing private property. Such expectations are particularly likely with regard to law-enforcement officers, who are perceived as law-abiding role models more often than as scofflaws. It is therefore reasonable, the courts should find, for a person to expect that police officers, charged as they are with upholding the law, will not violate any laws, including property and privacy laws, in doing so.

Rely on Legislation to Protect Privacy

The second-prong of *Katz* requires that the expectation of privacy be one that society is prepared to accept as legitimate. Basing the privacy interest on legislation, I submit, makes the interest per se legitimate. This interpretation of *Katz* would give legislatures, both state and federal, the power to expand at any time the rights guaranteed by the Fourth Amendment, simply by passing statutes of general applicability. A statute prohibiting your neighbor from peering into your house using Millivision [a high-tech concealed weapons detector] for example, would prohibit the police from doing the same (in the absence of a warrant). Of course, this would mean that the repeal of any property statute would re-open a door for police to operate. But the Supreme Court's current Fourth Amendment jurisprudence, protecting the home above (almost) all, would be used as a baseline, beneath which a mischievous state legislature would not be permitted to dip.

This proposal would have a significant impact. Under the current regime, evidence obtained by police without a warrant in violation of local property law is not necessarily excluded from admission at trial. Under a regime that defines the scope of the Fourth Amendment to be coextensive with the protections afforded by such local property laws, any evidence obtained without a warrant in violation of those laws would be obtained in violation of the Constitution itself, and thus inadmissible. If it is unreasonable as a matter of law for an ordinary citizen to violate a statute of general applicability, the same should be true of those whom society charges to uphold the law—police officers.

For all of its faults, the "reasonable expectation of privacy" test which *Katz v. United States* gave us to determine at what point the Fourth Amendment's protection attach is here to stay. By incorporating into the definition of "reasonable" a recognition of the central role that property law has played in the development of our legal system, the courts can ensure that the Constitution's protections will remain vital in the twenty-first century, regardless of what surveillance technologies the nation's law-enforcement agencies may develop.

> "[Katz] *changed dramatically the vo-*
> *cabulary we use when we talk about*
> *[Fourth Amendment] coverage."*

Katz Changed the Meaning of the Fourth Amendment

Charles E. Moylan Jr.

Charles E. Moylan Jr. is a former judge on the Maryland Court of Special Appeals. In the following selection, he describes the impact that the Katz v. United States *decision had on the interpretation of the Fourth Amendment, which protects citizens against unreasonable searches and seizures. He contends that the main effect of the* Katz *decision stemmed from the concurring opinion by John Marshall Harlan. In attempting to define the scope of the protection afforded by the Fourth Amendment, Harlan used the phrase "reasonable expectation of privacy." The introduction of this phrase, and the* Katz *decision in general, did not significantly change the extent of protection provided by the Fourth Amendment, according to Moylan. However, by changing the language used to describe the Fourth Amendment right, the* Katz *decision led to more flexibility in protecting people against unreasonable searches and seizures.*

The 1967 decision of *Katz v. United States* has arguably had a greater impact on the Fourth Amendment than any other single Supreme Court decision with the exception of *Mapp v. Ohio* (1961). Its impact, however, has been exclusively on the subject of threshold applicability or coverage. It may not have altered the substantive law with respect to coverage, but it has changed dramatically the vocabulary we use when we talk about coverage. The special impact of *Katz*, moreover, has proceeded not from the majority opinion of the Court but from the concurring opinion of Justice [John Marshall] Harlan. That concurrence, however, has been cited and quoted with approval so regularly by subsequent decisions of the Supreme Court that it has ripened into the majority position.

The Facts of the Case

The factual issue in *Katz* was a narrow one. FBI agents had warrantlessly placed an electronic eavesdropping device on the roof of a public telephone booth in Los Angeles, California. By the use of that "bug," they recorded the voice of Charles Katz as he illegally transmitted wagering information to contacts in Miami and Boston. There was no issue as to satisfaction of the Fourth Amendment for it was clear that the FBI agents, with ample time to have obtained a court order for the placement of the listening device, had not done so. If the Fourth Amendment applied, therefore, it had been violated. The only issue was that of whether the Fourth Amendment even covered the situation.

The earlier Supreme Court precedents of *Olmstead v. United States* (1928) and *Goldman v. United States* (1942) had held that there was no Fourth Amendment involvement unless there was a physical penetration into the constitutionally protected area. The electronic listening device at issue, like the one found to have been unoffending in *Goldman*, was one that did not penetrate the structure and did not, therefore, invade the constitutionally protected area. That distinction the Supreme Court repudiated, expressly overruling *Olmstead* and *Goldman* to the extent to which they had held a physical penetration into the constitutionally protected area the sine qua non of Fourth Amendment involvement. To do so, however, the Supreme Court had to change the way in which it described Fourth Amendment coverage.

Enhanced Fourth Amendment Protection

The *Katz* decision itself, confined to its factual context, was straightforward and free of confusion. The at-times-broad language of the *Katz* opinion, however, generated significant confusion and debate. Some argued that the very concept of a constitutionally protected perimeter was dead and that Fourth Amendment coverage had moved from inside that traditional perimeter to the broad outside. The predicate for that notion was the seven words early in the majority opinion, "the Fourth Amendment protects people, not places." Arguing against a too hasty conclusion that the very concept of "place" had lost its significance was the follow-up reference in the majority opinion, two paragraphs after the first, in which it stated, "the Fourth Amendment protects people—and not *simply* 'areas'" (emphasis supplied). Justice Harlan's concurrence, moreover, carefully pointed out:

> As the Court's opinion states, "the Fourth Amendment protects people, not places." The question, however, is what protection it affords to those people. Generally, as here, the answer to that question requires reference to a "place."

The opposite reading of the *Katz* decision in this regard was that it had not moved Fourth Amendment coverage from inside the traditionally protected area to the broad outside, for those were not the facts of *Katz*, but that it had, rather, *enhanced the quality of the protection* within the constitutionally protected perimeter. Justice Harlan's concurrence pointed out that for the period of its use and occupancy "an enclosed telephone booth is an area where, like a home," a person enjoys Fourth Amendment protection and is "unlike a field" where there is no such protection. That reading of *Katz* was that within the protected telephone booth, the thing protected was the privacy of the person inside the place and not the structural integrity of the "place" itself—the woodwork, the stucco, the glass. That, it was argued, was the intended meaning of protecting "people, not places." In repudiating *Olmstead* and *Goldman*, therefore, the Supreme Court had ruled that it was protecting a person inside such a protected area from such highly sophisticated intrusive, but non-penetrating, devices as laser beams and parabolic microphones and detecta-phones, just as traditionally it had protected against such old-fashioned penetrating devices as jimmies and crowbars and spike-mikes.

The debate between the two positions posed the classic law school issue of what is the law of the case when the decision itself, on its facts, is narrow, but where the language of the opinion announcing the decision is broad. In 1984, the well-reasoned analysis of Justice [Lewis] Powell in *Oliver v. United States* [which ruled that there is no Fourth Amendment protection in open fields] settled the debate in favor of the narrower interpretation, pointing out that that was the only interpretation that had a base in the actual facts of the *Katz* case itself.

"A Reasonable Expectation of Privacy"

The more far-reaching impact of *Katz* has stemmed from the concurring opinion of Justice Harlan. In groping for a way to describe Fourth Amendment coverage, he came up with the phrase "a reasonable expectation of privacy." It caught on. He broke it down into two component parts—its subjective aspect and its objective aspect. It is initially required that an individual have an actual or subjective expectation of privacy. Thus, even in the otherwise protected venue of a man's home, "objects, activities, or statements that he exposes to the 'plain view' of others are not 'protected' because no intention to keep them to himself has been exhibited." In the years since the *Katz* opinion was promulgated, emphasis has shifted decidedly away from this subjective aspect of a reasonable expectation of privacy and onto the objective aspect.

Even if an individual has an actual, subjective expectation of privacy, that does not translate into a Fourth Amendment protection unless such expectation is also one that society has objectively recognized as reasonable. "Conversations in the open would not be protected against being overheard for the expectation of privacy under the circumstances would be unreasonable [Cf. *Hester v. United States*]." It is because of the critical significance of this objective aspect of "a reasonable expectation of privacy" that the impact of *Katz* on the threshold issue of Fourth Amendment coverage is revealed to be more linguistic than substantive.

New Words for Fourth Amendment Protection

Where one used to ask, "Did the defendant enjoy a Fourth Amendment protection?," one now asks, "Did the defendant possess a reasonable expectation of privacy?" These are two ways of saying precisely the same thing. A Fourth Amendment protection is defined as "a reasonable expectation of privacy." Either the Fourth Amendment protection directly or the objectively measured "reasonable expectation of privacy" are then determined by such traditional inquiries as

1. Was the place that was searched covered by the Fourth Amendment?
2. Was the searcher an agent of government?
3. Was it the defendant, and not someone else, who enjoyed the protection or the expectation and, therefore, has the standing to raise the question?
4. Was the type of police conduct in issue a "search" or "seizure" or was it something else not covered by the Fourth Amendment?

The net effect has been simply to move such traditional inquiries one step further down in the outline. What used to be

I. Was There a Fourth Amendment Protection?

  A. Coverage of Place

  B. Coverage of Searcher

  C. Coverage of Defendant

  D. Coverage of Type of Police Conduct might have become

I. Was There a "Reasonable Expectation of Privacy"?

  A. Subjectively

  B. Objectively

    1. Coverage of Place

    2. Coverage of Searcher

    3. Coverage of Defendant

    4. Coverage of Type of Police Conduct

The most significant effect of the substitution of the new "reasonable expectation of privacy" language seems to be that instead of measuring coverage mechanistically—on an "all or nothing" basis—we measure it more flexibly according to the "totality of the circumstances."

CHAPTER 4

The Power of the Police to Stop and Frisk

Case Overview

Terry v. Ohio (1968)

The Supreme Court ruled in *Terry v. Ohio* that a police officer could stop and search a suspect based on reasonable suspicion. The decision created a new test for search and seizure and loosed some of the restrictions placed on police officers by not requiring a warrant for every search.

The case stemmed from an incident involving Cleveland police detective Martin McFadden, who observed three men acting strangely on a street corner. The three took turns walking back and forth on the street, looking in a store window and around the block, then pausing to speak with each other. McFadden did not have any evidence that a crime was to be committed other than his experience as a police officer and his observation of the suspects' behavior. Base on this observation, McFadden approached the men and questioned them. When one suspect, John W. Terry, did not answer his question, McFadden grabbed him, turned him around and patted down his coat. He found a revolver. Subsequent searches found a revolver in the coat of a second man, Richard Chilton.

At their trial for illegally carrying concealed weapons, Terry and Chilton filed a motion to prevent the guns from being used as evidence. They argued that Officer McFadden's search was unlawful because he had not obtained a warrant to search the suspects. The court rejected this motion, stating that there was reasonable cause for McFadden to believe the suspects were armed and that he had the right to protect himself by frisking them. Chilton and Terry were found guilty. Terry appealed his conviction, and the case was eventually brought to the Supreme Court on December 12, 1967.

In an 8-1 ruling on June 10, 1968, the Supreme Court upheld the conviction of Terry, deciding that Officer McFadden had acted reasonably in light of the circumstances. The Court argued that the Fourth Amendment does not protect the individual against all searches and seizures, but only against unreasonable ones. The Court then sought to determine if the search performed by McFadden was indeed reasonable. It put forth a description of what a reasonable stop and frisk would look like: The officer would observe suspicious activity and reasonably conclude a criminal act was about to be committed and that the suspects could be armed. He would then identify himself as a police officer and make reasonable inquiries to the suspects. If his initial fears that the suspects were armed were not allayed, he would then be entitled to conduct a carefully limited search of the outer clothing of the suspects to determine if they did indeed have weapons. The Court concluded that McFadden had followed this procedure and thus had conducted a proper search. Following this decision, the practice of stopping and frisking a suspect for weapons became known as a "Terry stop."

Terry v. Ohio created a gray area in law enforcement by allowing officers to act upon their suspicions in certain circumstances prior to obtaining a warrant. While previous rulings on searches and seizures, such as Mapp v. Ohio (1961) and Katz v. United States (1968), had placed a heavy burden on police officers by demanding warrants in most cases, the Terry case provided for a course of action that allowed the officers more freedom in stopping crime before it was committed.

> *"Where a police officer observes unusual conduct which leads him reasonably to conclude . . . that criminal activity may be afoot . . . he is entitled . . . to conduct a carefully limited search."*

The Court's Decision: With Reasonable Cause, Police May Stop and Search a Suspect

Earl Warren

The case of Terry v. Ohio *raised the question of whether the suspicion of a police officer meets the criteria for probable cause and therefore allows that officer to stop and frisk an individual. In the following excerpt from the majority opinion in the case, Chief Justice Earl Warren argues that Cleveland police officer Martin McFadden made a reasonable decision to search John W. Terry, whom he suspected of planning a robbery. Specifically, the circumstances and the actions observed by McFadden led him to reach the sound conclusion, according to the Court, that the suspect was armed and that the public's safety was at risk. Given such circumstances, a search is constitutional, and any weapon yielded by the search is admissible as evidence against the suspect in court. This ruling established the legality of the practice now known as a Terry stop, in which police officers stop suspicious persons and pat them down for weapons.*

Earl Warren served as chief justice of the Supreme Court from 1953 to 1969. His time on the Court saw many landmark civil rights cases as well as the Miranda v. Arizona *case,*

Earl Warren, majority opinion, *Terry v. Ohio* , June 10, 1968.

which outlined the rights of those being questioned in a criminal investigation.

The Fourth Amendment provides that "the right of the people to be secure in their persons, houses, papers, and effects, against unreasonable searches and seizures, shall not be violated. . . ." This inestimable right of personal security belongs as much to the citizen on the streets of our cities as to the homeowner closeted in his study to dispose of his secret affairs. For, as this Court has always recognized,

> No right is held more sacred, or is more carefully guarded, by the common law, than the right of every individual to the possession and control of his own person, free from all restraint or interference of others, unless by clear and unquestionable authority of law. *Union Pac. R. Co. v. Botsford* (1891).

We have recently held that "the Fourth Amendment protects people, not places," *Katz v. United States* (1967), and wherever an individual may harbor a reasonable "expectation of privacy" he is entitled to be free from unreasonable governmental intrusion. Of course, the specific content and incidents of this right must be shaped by the context in which it is asserted. For "what the Constitution forbids is not all searches and seizures, but unreasonable searches and seizures." *Elkins v. United States* (1960). Unquestionably petitioner [Terry] was entitled to the protection of the Fourth Amendment as he walked down the street in Cleveland. The question is whether in all the circumstances of this on-the-street encounter, his right to personal security was violated by an unreasonable search and seizure.

Troublesome Issues

We would be less than candid if we did not acknowledge that this question thrusts to the fore difficult and troublesome issues regarding a sensitive area of police activity—issues which have never before been squarely presented to this Court. Reflective of the tensions involved are the practical and constitutional arguments pressed with great vigor on both sides of the public debate over the power of the police to "stop and frisk"—as it is sometimes euphemistically termed—suspicious persons.

On the one hand, it is frequently argued that in dealing with the rapidly unfolding and often dangerous situations on city streets the police are in need of an escalating set of flexible responses, graduated in relation to the amount of information they possess. For this purpose it is urged that distinctions should be made between a "stop" and an "arrest" (or a "seizure" of a person), and between a "frisk" and a "search." Thus, it is argued, the police should be allowed to "stop" a person and detain him briefly for questioning upon suspicion that he may be connected with criminal activity. Upon suspicion that the person may be armed, the police should have the power to "frisk" him for weapons. If the "stop" and the "frisk" give rise to probable cause to believe that the suspect has committed a crime, then the police should be empowered to make a formal "arrest," and a full incident "search" of the person. This scheme is justified in part upon the notion that a "stop" and a "frisk" amount to a mere minor inconvenience and petty indignity [*People v. Rivero*] which can properly be imposed upon the citizen in the interest of effective law enforcement on the basis of a police officer's suspicion.

On the other side the argument is made that the authority of the police must be strictly circumscribed by the law of arrest and search as it has developed to date in the traditional jurisprudence of the Fourth Amendment. It is contended with some force that there is not—and cannot be—a variety of police activity which does not depend solely upon the voluntary cooperation of the citizen and yet which stops short of an arrest based upon probable cause to make such an arrest. The heart of the Fourth Amendment, the argument runs, is a severe requirement of specific justification for any intrusion upon protected personal security, coupled with a highly developed system of judicial controls to enforce upon the agents of the State the commands of the Constitution. Acquiescence by the courts in the compulsion inherent in the field interrogation practices at issue here, it is urged, would constitute an abdication of judicial control over, and indeed an encouragement of, substantial interference with liberty and personal security by police officers whose judgment is necessarily colored by their primary involvement in "the often competitive enterprise of ferreting out crime." *Johnson v. United States* (1948). This, it is argued, can only serve to exacerbate police-community tensions in the crowded centers of our Nation's cities. . . .

Is a Stop and Frisk Reasonable?

Having thus roughly sketched the perimeters of the constitutional debate over the limits on police investigative conduct in general and the background against which this case presents itself, we turn our attention to the quite narrow question posed by the facts before us: whether it is always unreasonable for a policeman to seize a person and subject him to a limited search for weapons unless there is probable cause for an arrest. Given the narrowness of this question, we have no occasion to canvass in detail the constitutional limitations upon the scope of a policeman's power when he confronts a citizen without probable cause to arrest him.

Our first task is to establish at what point in this encounter the Fourth Amendment becomes relevant. That is, we must decide whether and when Officer McFadden "seized" Terry and whether and when he conducted a "search." There is some suggestion in the use of such terms as "stop" and "frisk" that such police conduct is outside the purview of the Fourth Amendment because neither action rises to the level of a "search" or "seizure" within the meaning of the Constitution. We emphatically reject this notion. It is quite plain that the Fourth Amendment governs "seizures" of the person which do not eventuate in a trip to the station house and prosecution for crime—"arrests" in traditional terminology. It must be recognized that whenever a police officer accosts an individual and restrains his freedom to walk away, he has "seized" that person. And it is nothing less than sheer torture of the English language to suggest that a careful exploration of the outer surfaces of a person's clothing all over his or her body in an attempt to find weapons is not a "search." Moreover, it is simply fantastic to urge that such a procedure performed in public by a policeman while the citizen stands helpless, perhaps facing a wall with his hands raised, is a "petty indignity." It is a serious intrusion upon the sanctity of the person, which may inflict great indignity and arouse strong resentment, and it is not to be undertaken lightly.

Scope of a Search Must Be Justified

The danger in the logic which proceeds upon distinctions between a "stop" and an "arrest," or "seizure" of the person, and between a "frisk" and a "search" is two-fold. It seeks to isolate from constitutional scrutiny the initial stages of the contact between the policeman and the citizen. And by suggesting a rigid all-or-nothing model of justification and regulation under the Amendment, it obscures the utility of limitations upon the scope, as well as the initiation, of police action as a means of constitutional regulation. This Court has held in the past that a search which is reasonable at its inception may violate the Fourth Amendment by virtue of its intolerable intensity and scope. The scope of the search must be "strictly tied to and justified by" the circumstances which rendered its initiation permissible. *Warden v. Hayden* (1967).

The distinctions of classical "stop-and-frisk" theory thus serve to divert attention from the central inquiry under the

Fourth Amendment—the reasonableness in all the circumstances of the particular governmental invasion of a citizen's personal security. "Search" and "seizure" are not talismans. We therefore reject the notions that the Fourth Amendment does not come into play at all as a limitation upon police conduct if the officers stop short of something called a "technical arrest" or a "full-blown search."

In this case there can be no question, then, that Officer McFadden "seized" petitioner and subjected him to a "search" when he took hold of him and patted down the outer surfaces of his clothing. We must decide whether at that point it was reasonable for Officer McFadden to have interfered with petitioner's personal security as he did. And in determining whether the seizure and search were "unreasonable" our inquiry is a dual one—whether the officer's action was justified at its inception, and whether it was reasonably related in scope to the circumstances which justified the interference in the first place. . . .

The Conduct of the Officer

We must now examine the conduct of Officer McFadden in this case to determine whether his search and seizure of petitioner were reasonable, both at their inception and as conducted. He had observed Terry, together with [Richard] Chilton and another man [Katz], acting in a manner he took to be preface to a "stick-up." We think on the facts and circumstances Officer McFadden detailed before the trial judge a reasonably prudent man would have been warranted in believing petitioner was armed and thus presented a threat to the officer's safety while he was investigating his suspicious behavior. The actions of Terry and Chilton were consistent with McFadden's hypothesis that these men were contemplating a daylight robbery—which, it is reasonable to assume, would be likely to involve the use of weapons—and nothing in their conduct from the time he first noticed them until the time he confronted them and identified himself as a police officer gave him sufficient reason to negate that hypothesis. Although the trio had departed the original scene, there was nothing to indicate abandonment of an intent to commit a robbery at some point. Thus, when Officer McFadden approached the three men gathered before the display window at Zucker's store he had observed enough to make it quite reasonable to fear that they were armed; and nothing in their response to his hailing them, identifying himself as a police officer, and asking their names served to dispel that reasonable belief. We cannot say his decision at that point to seize Terry and pat his clothing for weapons was the product of a volatile or inventive imagination, or was undertaken simply as an act of harassment; the record evidences the tempered act of a policeman who in the course of an investigation had to make a quick decision as to how to protect himself and others from possible danger, and took limited steps to do so.

The manner in which the seizure and search were conducted is, of course, as vital a part of the inquiry as whether they were warranted at all. The Fourth Amendment proceeds as much by limitations upon the scope of governmental action as by imposing preconditions upon its initiation. The entire deterrent purpose of the rule excluding evidence seized in violation of the Fourth Amendment rests on the assumption that "limitations upon the fruit to be gathered tend to limit the quest itself." *United States v. Poller* (1930). Thus, evidence may not be introduced if it was discovered by means of a seizure and search which were not reasonably related in scope to the justification for their initiation.

Not a Problematic Search

We need not develop at length in this case, however, the limitations which the Fourth Amendment places upon a protective seizure and search for weapons. These limitations will have to be developed in the concrete factual circumstances of individual cases. Suffice it to note that such a search, unlike a search without a warrant incident to a lawful arrest, is not justified by any need to prevent the disappearance or destruction of evidence of crime. The sole justification of the search in the present situation is the protection of the police officer and others nearby, and it must therefore be confined in scope to an intrusion reasonably designed to discover guns, knives, clubs, or other hidden instruments for the assault of the police officer.

The scope of the search in this case presents no serious problem in light of these standards. Officer McFadden patted down the outer clothing of petitioner and his two companions. He did not place his hands in their pockets or under the outer surface of their garments until he had felt weapons, and then he merely reached for and removed the guns. He never did invade Katz' person beyond the outer surfaces of his clothes, since he discovered nothing in his pat-down which might have been a weapon. Officer McFadden confined his search strictly to what was minimally necessary to learn whether the men were armed and to disarm them once he discovered the weapons. He did not conduct a general exploratory search for whatever evidence of criminal activity he might find.

We conclude that the revolver seized from Terry was properly admitted in evidence against him. At the time he seized petitioner and searched him for weapons, Officer McFadden had reasonable grounds to believe that petitioner was armed and dangerous, and it was necessary for the protection of himself and others to take swift measures to discover the true facts and neutralize the threat of harm if it materialized. The policeman carefully restricted his search to what was appropriate to the discovery of the particular items which he sought. Each case of this sort will, of course, have to be decided on its own facts. We merely hold today that where a police officer observes unusual conduct which leads him reasonably to conclude in light of his experience that criminal activity may be afoot and that the persons with whom he is dealing may be armed and presently dangerous, where in the course of investigating this behavior he identifies himself as a policeman and makes reasonable inquiries, and where nothing in the initial stages of the encounter serves to dispel his reasonable fear for his own or others' safety, he is entitled for the protection of himself and others in the area to conduct a carefully limited search of the outer clothing of such persons in an attempt to discover weapons which might be used to assault him. Such a search is a reasonable search under the Fourth Amendment, and any weapons seized may properly be introduced in evidence against the person from whom they were taken.

> "If the individual is no longer to be sov-
> ereign . . . , if [police] can 'seize' and
> 'search' him in their discretion, we en-
> ter a new regime."

Dissenting Opinion: *Terry* Is a Dangerous Expansion of Probable Cause

William O. Douglas

Terry v. Ohio *changed the balance between the rights of a private citizen and the power of the police to enforce the law. The
lawyer for John W. Terry, the petitioner, held that simply observing a person behaving suspiciously was not probable cause for a
police officer to stop and search that person. The majority of the
Supreme Court disagreed and ruled that the police did indeed
have the power to stop someone based solely on the observations
of the officer at the scene. However, there were those in the
Court who disagreed and who saw this case as an erosion of personal privacy.*

*Justice William O. Douglas wrote the dissent in this case. In
his dissent, excerpted here, he focuses on the concept of probable
cause. He argues that the opinion of a police officer that someone looks as if they are going to commit a crime and that they
may be armed does not justify detaining and searching that person. He states that the police should be held to a stricter interpretation of probable cause. If they are not, he reasons, the rights
of citizens will be severely compromised.*

*Douglas is the longest-serving Supreme Court justice in his-
tory. He was sworn in on April 17, 1939, and served until*

William O. Douglas, dissenting opinion, *Terry v. Ohio*, June 10, 1968.

*his retirement on November 12, 1975, following a stroke. Dou-
glas was known as a strong supporter of individual rights, and
he called for a literal interpretation of the freedom of speech
found in the First Amendment.*

I agree that petitioner was "seized" within the meaning of
the Fourth Amendment. I also agree that frisking petitioner
and his companions for guns was a "search." But it is a mys-
tery how that "search" and that "seizure" can be constitutional
by Fourth Amendment standards, unless there was "probable
cause" to believe that (1) a crime had been committed or (2)
a crime was in the process of being committed or (3) a crime
was about to be committed.

The opinion of the Court disclaims the existence of "probable cause." If loitering were in issue and that was the offense
charged, there would be "probable cause" shown. But the
crime here is carrying concealed weapons; and there is no basis for concluding that the officer had "probable cause" for believing that that crime was being committed. Had a warrant
been sought, a magistrate would, therefore, have been unauthorized to issue one, for he can act only if there is a showing
of "probable cause." We [therefore] hold today that the police
have greater authority to make a "seizure" and conduct a
"search" than a judge has to authorize such action. [Yet, until
now] we have said precisely the opposite over and over again.

Reasonable Suspicion Is Not Probable Cause

In other words, police officers up to today have been permitted to effect arrests or searches without warrants only when
the facts within their personal knowledge would satisfy the
constitutional standard of probable cause. At the time of their
"seizure" without a warrant they must possess facts concern-
ing the person arrested that would have satisfied a magistrate
that "probable cause" was indeed present. The term "probable
cause" rings a bell of certainty that is not sounded by phrases

such as "reasonable suspicion." Moreover, the meaning of "probable cause" is deeply imbedded in our constitutional history. As we stated in *Henry v. United States* [1959]:

> The requirement of probable cause has roots that are deep in our history. The general warrant, in which the name of the person to be arrested was left blank, and the writs of assistance, against which James Otis inveighed, both perpetuated the oppressive practice of allowing the police to arrest and search on suspicion. Police control took the place of judicial control, since no showing of "probable cause" before a magistrate was required....
>
> That philosophy [rebelling against these practices] later was reflected in the Fourth Amendment. And as the early American decisions both before and immediately after its adoption show, common rumor or report, suspicion, or even "strong reason to suspect" was not adequate to support a warrant for arrest. And that principle has survived to this day....
>
> It is important, we think, that this requirement [of probable cause] be strictly enforced, for the standard set by the Constitution protects both the officer and the citizen. If the officer acts with probable cause, he is protected even though it turns out that the citizen is innocent.... And while a search without a warrant is, within limits, permissible if incident to a lawful arrest, if an arrest without a warrant is to support an incidental search, it must be made with probable cause.... This immunity of officers cannot fairly be enlarged without jeopardizing the privacy or security of the citizen.

A Step Down the Totalitarian Path

The infringement on personal liberty of any "seizure" of a person can only be "reasonable" under the Fourth Amendment if we require the police to possess "probable cause" before they seize him. Only that line draws a meaningful distinction between an officer's mere inkling and the presence of facts within the officer's personal knowledge which would convince a reasonable man that the person seized has committed, is committing, or is about to commit a particular crime. "In dealing with probable cause, . . . as the very name implies, we deal with probabilities. These are not technical; they are the factual and practical considerations of everyday life on which reasonable and prudent men, not legal technicians, act." *Brinegar v. United States* [1949].

To give the police greater power than a magistrate is to take a long step down the totalitarian path. Perhaps such a step is desirable to cope with modern forms of lawlessness. But if it is taken, it should be the deliberate choice of the people through a constitutional amendment. Until the Fourth Amendment, which is closely allied with the Fifth, is rewritten, the person and the effects of the individual are beyond the reach of all government agencies until there are reasonable grounds to believe (probable cause) that a criminal venture has been launched or is about to be launched.

There have been powerful hydraulic pressures throughout our history that bear heavily on the Court to water down constitutional guarantees and give the police the upper hand. That hydraulic pressure has probably never been greater than it is today.

Yet if the individual is no longer to be sovereign, if the police can pick him up whenever they do not like the cut of his jib, if they can "seize" and "search" him in their discretion, we enter a new regime. The decision to enter it should be made only after a full debate by the people of this country.

> *"The* Terry *decision only authorizes action upon* reasonable *suspicion of criminality and a frisking* reasonably *necessary for the officer's protection."*

The Power Provided by *Terry* Must Be Used Responsibly

Fred E. Inbau and James R. Thompson

One of the central questions in the case of Terry v. Ohio *was how much leeway the police have in executing a stop and frisk— stopping an individual who is not committing a crime and searching him or her for possible weapons. The Supreme Court ruled that if police officers observe an individual acting in a suspicious manner, it is in their power to stop that person and frisk them for weapons.*

In the following selection, written shortly after the Court reached its decision in 1968, Fred E. Inbau and James R. Thompson agree with the ruling. However, they call on the police to use the newly granted power justly and cautiously. While agreeing that this ruling gives the police an important weapon in preventing crime, they also realize there is a great potential for abuse in its application. By placing the burden of probable cause in the hands of a police officer in the heat of the moment, the Court has given corrupt officers the power to intimidate and harass with impunity. Inbau and Thompson implore the police departments to train their officers appropriately so that this new weapon will be handled with care.

Fred E. Inbau taught law at Northwestern University in Evanston, Illinois, specializing in criminal justice, particularly in the area of police interrogation. He founded Americans for Effective Law Enforcement (AELE) to support the efforts of the police and to petition the courts on their behalf.

James R. Thompson helped to found the AELE and served as its first president. Thompson later served as U.S. attorney and then as the governor of Illinois for four terms.

On June 10 [1968] the Supreme Court of the United States, in the case of *Terry v. Ohio*, rendered a decision that will greatly aid the police in their efforts to prevent crime and apprehend criminals. That decision, however, must not be interpreted by the police as a green light for indiscriminate, arbitrary stopping and frisking, or for any other unworthy purpose.

Americans for Effective Law Enforcement, Inc. [AELE], a non-partisan, non-political, not-for-profit educational corporation, which was founded ... for the purpose of advancing the cause of effective law enforcement, filed an "amicus curiae" (friend of the Court) brief in the *Terry* case last November [1967]. It urged the Court to rule as it did.

A New Power and Guidelines for Police

Upon the reasonable assumption that our brief had a persuasive effect upon the Supreme Court, we feel privileged to now admonish the police to assume the proper *responsibility* that must accompany this *privilege* so newly sanctioned by the Court.

The *Terry* decision only authorizes action upon *reasonable* suspicion of criminality and a frisking *reasonably* necessary for the officer's protection. And all this must be performed in a *reasonable* manner.

The Court's opinion sets up general guidelines for the police. The actual holding of the case, however, indicates that the

Court intended to confine the power to "stop" to situations which clearly call for investigation of criminally suspicious circumstances and the power of "frisk" to situations where there is a probability that the person to be frisked or searched is armed and may be dangerous to the officer or other citizens. The Court said:

> ... where a police officer observes unusual conduct which leads him reasonably to conclude in light of his experience that criminal activity may be afoot and that the persons with whom he is dealing may be armed and presently dangerous; where in the course of investigating this behavior he identifies himself as a policeman and makes reasonable inquiries; and where nothing in the initial stages of the encounter serves to dispel his reasonable fear for his own or others' safety, he is entitled for the protection of himself and others in the area to conduct a carefully limited search of the outer clothing of such persons in an attempt to discover weapons which might be used to assault him. Such a search is a reasonable search under the Fourth Amendment, and any weapons seized may properly be introduced in evidence against the person from whom they were taken.

Of course, the decision is not limited to the kind of facts set out in the *Terry* case. It encompasses a variety of suspicious conduct which the police meet every day during the course of field investigation and interrogation. For this reason, police training schools and police legal advisors must relay the message of the Court in meaningful terms to the police officer, with the use of appropriate examples of what is and what is not reasonable action in stop and frisk situations. Reference to the Court's holding, however, makes it unmistakably clear that the Court will not tolerate "dragnet" seizures and frisks which, though designed to achieve ostensibly worthy objectives, e.g., gun control or harassment of vice offenders and juvenile gangs, do not measure up to the Fourth Amendment requirement of reasonableness.

This Power Can Be Easily Abused

By its decision in the *Terry* case, the Supreme Court delivered into the hands of the police a very powerful weapon for the prevention and detection of crime. This power, however, is readily subject to abuse by an ignorant, brutal, or corrupt police officer. And any abuse of the power may easily lead to deterioration of [the] police-citizen relationship, especially in the tense and emotionally charged slum areas of our large cities. All measures necessary to prevent this abuse must be taken by those in command positions within the police force itself.

AELE is proud of the effort it made in the *Terry* case to persuade the Supreme Court to uphold the right of the police to "stop and frisk." In our brief we pledged the Court that law enforcement agencies would not abuse the power we requested the Court to sanction. We now ask that the police of this country make good our word, and that they proceed to exercise their newly won legitimate power with tolerance, understanding, tact, and caution. What the Supreme Court has granted, the legislatures can take away upon evidence of police abuse of that power.

How well the police use the power may play an important part in future cases coming before the courts in which they are asked to rule in favor of the needs of law enforcement. This factor may also shape the course of events in the halls of Congress and before other legislative bodies whenever proposals are under consideration for additional grants of police powers.

We urge the police to use well and fairly the power they now clearly have, for the protection and preservation of the rights of all citizens.

"The Court stripped away the racial dimension of the case by removing all references to the participants' race."

Terry Had an Unstated Racial Dimension

Anthony C. Thompson

Anthony C. Thompson is a professor of clinical law at New York University School of Law. He has worked as a criminal defense attorney and a public defender and has written several articles dealing with criminal justice.

In the following article Thompson argues that the issue of race played a major role in the Terry *case. The detective in the case, Martin McFadden, was white, and two of the three suspects he stopped and frisked (including John Terry) were African Americans—although the Court makes no reference to this fact in the decision or the dissent. Thompson suggests that McFadden's reason for initially suspecting Terry may have been based on race. The Court then omitted any reference to race and instead stressed McFadden's police expertise in order to establish grounds for a reasonable search and seizure. In addition, Thompson contends that the* Terry *ruling makes it clear that the Supreme Court deems itself powerless to control rogue police officers who may abuse the stop and frisk practice in order to unjustly harass minorities.*

The Supreme Court's decision in *Terry v. Ohio* is well known for the Fourth Amendment rule it announced: The police can conduct limited seizures of the person (now

Anthony C. Thompson, "Stopping the Usual Suspects: Race and the Fourth Amendment," *New York University Law Review*, vol. 74, October 1, 1999. Copyright © 1999 by *New York University Law Review*. Reproduced by permission.

commonly known as "Terry stops") and limited patdowns of a person ("Terry frisks") based on a quantum of suspicion that is less substantial than the "probable cause" standard that the police must satisfy when conducting full-blown arrests and equivalent seizures of the person. In reading the decision, one would see no reason to view the case as relevant to the issue of racially motivated searches and seizures. Yet, closer review of the case—especially when supplemented with an examination of the briefs and the trial court record in the case—reveals an important racial dimension.

In the majority opinion's statement of facts, Chief Justice [Earl] Warren described Detective Martin McFadden's observations of two men, John Terry and Richard Chilton, standing on a street corner in "downtown Cleveland." There is no mention of the race of any of these individuals. The decision states that McFadden "had never seen the two men before, and he was unable to say precisely what first drew his eye to them." McFadden (who was in plain clothes) watched first one individual, then the other, walk back and forth in front of a store window and look in the window as they passed. At one point in this sequence of events, as the two individuals were standing together on the corner, "a third man approached them and engaged them briefly in conversation" then "left the two others and walked west on Euclid Avenue"; after again "pacing, peering, and conferring," Chilton and Terry headed "west on Euclid Avenue, following the path taken earlier by the third man." The Court's decision also does not mention the race of "the third man."

Having concluded that Chilton and Terry were in the process of "'casing a job, a stick-up,'" McFadden followed them down the street. He observed them "stop . . . to talk to the same man who had conferred with them earlier on the street corner." "Deciding that the situation was ripe for direct action," McFadden approached the group, identified himself as a police officer and asked for their names. The men "'mumbled something' in response to [the officer's] inquiries," which caused the officer to "grab [petitioner] Terry, spin him around so they were facing the other two, ... and pat down the outside of his clothing." Finding a gun on Terry, the officer patted down the other two and also found a gun in Chilton's overcoat.

The Issue of Race Was Absent in the Court's Discussion

The Court presented the foregoing facts, which represent the key portions of the *Terry* opinion's factual presentation, in entirely race-neutral terms. When treatises recite the facts of *Terry*, they generally follow the Court's lead. But an examination of the trial court record reveals that John Terry and Richard Chilton were African American; "the third man," Katz, was white; Detective McFadden also was white.

The Court's legal analysis was almost entirely devoid of references to race. Invoking an approach to the Fourth Amendment previously used in the context of administrative searches, the Court explained that it was diverging from the strict "probable cause" standard and instead adopting a lesser "reasonableness" standard as the measure for brief on-the-street seizures of the person and attendant patdowns of their clothing. The Court's discussion focused almost exclusively on doctrinal aspects of Fourth Amendment law and practical considerations in adapting Fourth Amendment rules to "the need for law enforcement officers to protect themselves and other prospective victims of violence."

In one sentence of the opinion and an accompanying footnote, the Court addressed the subject of race. In the textual passage, the Court observed that "minority groups, particularly Negroes, frequently complain" of "wholesale harassment by certain elements of the police community." The accompanying footnote acknowledged:

> The frequency with which "frisking" forms a part of field in-
> terrogation practice ... cannot help but be a severely exacer-
> bating factor in police-community tensions, ... particularly
> ... in situations where the "stop and frisk" of youths or mi-
> nority group members is "motivated by the officers' per-
> ceived need to maintain the power image of the beat of-
> ficer."

But the Court dismissed these considerations from its analysis
of the Fourth Amendment issues presented by the case, stating
summarily that a rule requiring suppression would not prevent improper police activity of this sort.

The Issue of Racially Motivated Stops

The *Terry* opinion's brief discussion of race presumably was a
response to an amicus curiae brief filed by the NAACP [Na-
tional Association for the Advancement of Colored People]
Legal Defense and Educational Fund. In that brief, the Legal
Defense Fund cited statistics showing that blacks were more
prone to being stopped and frisked than whites. Observing
that "many thousands of our citizens who have been or may
be stopped and interrogated yearly, only to be released when
the police find them innocent of any crime," the Legal Defense
Fund warned that the police would exploit a diluted probable
cause standard to engage in exploratory searches under the
guise of protecting themselves.

Justice [William O.] Douglas's strongly worded dissent in
Terry echoed some of the themes sounded by the Legal Defense Fund's brief. He declared that the majority's conferral
upon the police of expanded powers of search and seizure
represented "a long step down the totalitarian path." Given
what he called the "hydraulic pressures" of society to diminish
constitutional guarantees, he predicted that the nation was
now entering a "new regime" in which police officers could
pick up an individual "whenever they did not like the cut of
his jib." Yet, Justice Douglas did not advert to the racial di-

mension of these concerns as identified in the Legal Defense Fund's brief or in any other way refer to considerations of race.

When one adds the missing racial element to the Court's statement of facts, certain otherwise inexplicable events suddenly become much more comprehensible. Detective McFadden's assertion that "he was unable to say precisely what first drew his eye to [Terry and Chilton]," an assertion accepted by the trial court and uncritically recited by the Supreme Court, assumes a new meaning when one views *Terry* as a case in which a white detective noticed—and then focused his attention on—two black men who were doing nothing more than standing on a street corner in downtown Cleveland in the middle of the afternoon. The Court quoted Detective McFadden's statement that "'they didn't look right to me at the time,'" but gave no explanation for what "'didn't look right'" meant to McFadden because he himself had offered no such explanation in his testimony.

The Arresting Officer Recounts the Stop

With the element of race restored to the case, it is more readily apparent why these two men "didn't look right" to him. This inference becomes even clearer when one considers the officer's elaboration on this point in his testimony at the trial:

Well, at what point did you consider their actions unusual?

Well, to be truthful with you, I didn't like them. I was just attracted to them, and I surmised that there was something going on when one of them left the other one and did the walking up, walk up past the store and stopped and looked in and come back again.

Well, would this be a fair statement then, that it was at this point then that you decided you ought to watch them further?

Well, I will be truthful with you, I will stand and watch people or walk and watch people at many intervals of the day. Some people that don't look right to me, I will watch them. Now, in this case when I looked over they didn't look right to me at the time.

With the officer's "interest aroused," as the Court put it, everything the men did became suspicious. Their actions in walking back and forth past a store window and gazing into the store—which the Court itself acknowledged was not inherently suspicious since people routinely "stroll up and down the street" and "store windows . . . are made to be looked in"—became, in the officer's mind, symptomatic of an "elaborately casual and oft-repeated reconnaissance of the store window" for the purpose of "casing a job, a stick-up." Interestingly, one of the factors that aroused the officer's suspicions was that these two African American men conferred with a white man, who initially left and thereafter rejoined the group. In his suppression hearing testimony, the officer made a point of referring to the race of each of the participants when he described their contact with each other. The interracial nature of the group apparently also "didn't look right" to the detective. Based on these observations, the officer followed the three men, stopped them, demanded identification, and, "when the men 'mumbled something' in response to his inquiries, . . . grabbed petitioner Terry, spun him around . . . and patted down the outside of his clothing."

Racially Motivated Suspicions?

The Court stripped away the racial dimension of the case by removing all references to the participants' race. Although one cannot, of course, reconstruct the reasons for this rhetorical choice, it seems evident at least that this was a conscious choice. In his suppression hearing testimony, Detective McFadden repeatedly referred to the "third man" (Katz) as a "white man"; the lawyers who questioned McFadden did so as well. Yet, the Court's opinion refers to him only as "the third man" or by name.

The removal of race from the case presented the Court with a dilemma, however. To determine whether to uphold McFadden's actions under the new "stop and frisk" doctrine, the Court had to ascertain precisely why McFadden stopped and frisked Terry. After all, an essential element of pre-Terry "probable cause" doctrine—and one the Court carried forward to the new "stop and frisk" rule—was that a search and seizure had to be supported by specific facts that could be weighed by an objective magistrate. But, with race eliminated from the case, the most obvious explanation for McFadden's suspicions and his subsequent actions was unavailable. The Court was left with McFadden's testimony that "he was unable to say precisely what first drew his eye to them." McFadden's explanations for his subsequent actions in stopping and frisking Terry were not much better. He claimed to see criminality in Terry's and Chilton's actions of pacing back and forth in front of the store, gazing into the store window, and conferring with a third man—acts which the Court itself had to acknowledge were innocuous and hardly emblematic of criminal activity. The frisk, which under the Court's new standard had to be supported by reasonable suspicion that the individual is "armed and dangerous," seemed to be based upon utter speculation. Having concluded that the three men must be preparing to commit a daylight robbery, McFadden then deduced that they must be armed because a "daylight robbery . . . would be likely to involve the use of weapons."

"Police Officer as Expert"

What the Court did to "make sense" of McFadden's actions is best understood in the terms of narrative theory. As others have explained, a sound judicial opinion requires coherent factual and legal narratives. Such narratives permit the judges to clarify the events in their own minds and to present the facts and law in a manner that the legal community will generally accept. In Terry, the narrative upon which the Court settled was one of the "police officer as expert." To explain Detective McFadden's immediate distrust of the two men on the street corner, the Court stated:

> He had never seen the two men before, and he was unable to say precisely what first drew his eye to them. However, he testified that he had been a policeman for 39 years and a detective for 35 and that he had been assigned to patrol this vicinity of downtown Cleveland for shoplifters and pickpockets for 30 years. He explained . . . that he would "stand and watch people or walk and watch people at many intervals of the day." He added: "Now, in this case when I looked over they didn't look right to me at the time."

The Court took McFadden's statement that could easily be construed in racial terms ("they didn't look right to me") and transformed it into a highly skilled officer's instinctive assessment that something in the situation seemed awry and worthy of investigation. And the Court accomplished this transformation in a manner quite familiar to those who study narrative: not explicitly (which would have been impossible since McFadden's testimony lacked such a direct link) but by juxtaposing two apparently unconnected subjects.

After acknowledging that each of the acts observed by McFadden was "perhaps innocent in itself" and consistent with the actions of individuals who are not engaged in criminal activity, the Court invoked the expertise of the detective to declare that "it would have been poor police work indeed for an officer of 30 years' experience in the detection of thievery from stores in this same neighborhood to have failed to investigate this behavior further." To justify McFadden's additional intrusion of frisking Terry, the Court stated:

> We cannot say his decision . . . to seize Terry and pat his clothing for weapons was the product of a volatile or inventive imagination, or was undertaken simply as an act of harassment; the record evidences the tempered act of a police-

man who in the course of an investigation had to make a quick decision as to how to protect himself and others from possible danger, and took limited steps to do so.

Not a "Hunch"

An independent examination of McFadden's suppression hearing testimony provides cause to be skeptical of the Court's characterizations of his expertise. Of course, the Court in the *Terry* opinion does not claim for McFadden any experience in recognizing "casing," for the Court could not have done so. Instead, it implies such expertise by saying that McFadden "testified that he had been a policeman for 39 years and a detective for 35 and that he had been assigned to patrol this vicinity of downtown Cleveland for shoplifters and pickpockets for 30 years." The ultimate truth of the question of whether McFadden really was an expert hardly matters. As cognitive psychologist Jerome Bruner reminds us, "matters of fact, even when filtered through rules of evidence, oaths, and cross-examination, do not, after all, speak for themselves. In many ways, facts are constructed in response to value judgments that exist either in the broader society or in the law itself. . . ." The "police officer as expert" narrative allowed the Court in *Terry* to present a coherent, raceless narrative about why McFadden acted as he did. Moreover, and more important for the broader canvas of Fourth Amendment jurisprudence on which the Court was painting, this device permitted the Court to denounce judicial reliance on police "hunches" in a case in which the Court was doing the very thing it was nominally condemning. In a key passage of the *Terry* opinion, the Court stated, "in determining whether the officer acted reasonably . . . , due weight must be given, not to his inchoate and unparticularized suspicion or 'hunch,' but to the specific reasonable inferences which he is entitled to draw from the facts in light of his experience." The Court treated McFadden's largely unexplained suspicions as "the specific reasonable in ferences" of a highly "experienced" officer rather than a mere "hunch" by transforming McFadden into an expert.

In stripping away race from the case and substituting the officer-as-expert narrative, the Court in *Terry* essentially created a conceptual construct: an officer who was unaffected by considerations of race and who could be trusted even in a race-laden case like *Terry* to be acting on the basis of legitimate indicia of criminal activity. Such an officer could be trusted with the expanded powers conferred by the *Terry* opinion, notwithstanding the dire warnings of the [NAACP] Legal Defense Fund.

Racially Motivated Stop and Frisks Continue

Of course, even if the "Detective McFaddens" of the world could be trusted to perform in a race-neutral manner, that still left the other kind of officer described in the Legal Defense Fund brief: the officer who would abuse expanded search and seizure powers unjustly to stop and frisk African Americans and other members of "'unpopular racial and religious minorities.'" To deal with this concern, the Court once again constructed a narrative. This time, the Court's narrative focused on the Court itself describing the limits of judicial power, and specifically the limitations of lawmakers in construing the Fourth Amendment. The Court stated:

> The wholesale harassment by certain elements of the police community, of which minority groups, particularly Negroes, frequently complain, will not be stopped by the exclusion of any evidence from any criminal trial. Yet a rigid and unthinking application of the exclusionary rule in futile protest against practices which it can never be used effectively to control, may exact a high toll in human injury and frustration of efforts to prevent crime.

Although the Court in this passage appears to accept the validity of the complaints of "wholesale harassment" of "minority groups," the Court attributes these abuses to "certain elements of the police community." In essence, the Court divides the world of police officers into "good cops" (the "Detective McFaddens" of the world, who can be trusted) and "rogue cops" (the ones who might be expected to abuse whatever powers have been delegated to them). With respect to the latter group, the Court declares itself powerless—at least in the context of a case implicating the Fourth Amendment and the proper manner of applying the exclusionary rule—to exert control over their abuses. Any such effort, the Court asserts, would be "futile." Even if such a "futile protest" might have symbolic value, the Court concludes that such symbolism must be eschewed because the position advocated by the Legal Defense Fund (adherence to the preexisting probable cause standard) would unacceptably hamper police officers and put them at risk.

The foregoing is of course only a small part of the very large story of *Terry v. Ohio*. Much more can be said (and has been said by others) about, among other things, the facts of the case and the Court's legal analysis, the place of *Terry* in Fourth Amendment jurisprudence, and the political context of *Terry* and the extent to which that backdrop affected the Court's ruling and rhetoric. This take on *Terry*, however, offers some insights into the Court's treatment of racial motivation in Fourth Amendment cases.

Organizations to Contact

Academy of Criminal Justice Sciences (ACJS)
PO Box 960, Greenbelt, MD 20768-0960
(301) 446-6300
e-mail: ExecDir@acjs.org
Web site: www.acjs.org

The ACJS is an association that seeks to promote scholarly activity in the field of criminal justice. It provides education, research, and analysis for criminal justice professionals as well as educators and students. Publications include the three journals *Justice Quarterly (JQ)*, *Journal of Criminal Justice Education (JCJE)*, and *ACJS Today*.

American Bar Association (ABA)
321 N. Clark St., Chicago, IL 60610
(800) 285-2221
e-mail: askaba@abanet.org
Web site: www.abanet.org

The ABA is the national association of lawyers and law professionals. It seeks to promote public awareness of legal matters and professional ethics and conduct. It provides information on many cases as well as collections of online resources on a variety of legal topics.

American Civil Liberties Union (ACLU)
125 Broad St., 18th Fl., New York, NY 10004-2400
(212) 549-2500
e-mail: aclu@aclu.org
Web site: www.aclu.org

The ACLU is a national organization that works to defend civil rights as guaranteed in the Constitution. It publishes various materials on civil liberties, including the newsletter

Civil Liberties and a set of handbooks on individual rights. Its Web site features many articles on a number of current criminal justice issues.

Criminal Justice Legal Foundation (CJLF)
PO Box 1199, Sacramento, CA 95812
(916) 446-0345
e-mail: rushford@cjlf.org
Web site: www.cjlf.org

The CJLF works to protect the rights of victims of crimes and to promote stronger anticrime legislation. Resources on its Web site include a list of all the criminal justice cases the foundation has participated in as well as the results and case summaries of each case. It also publishes the *Advisory*, a quarterly newsletter.

National Criminal Justice Association (NCJA)
720 Seventh St. NW, 3rd Fl.
 Washington, DC 20001-3716
(202) 628-8550
Web site: www.ncja.org

The National Criminal Justice Association works to promote the development of criminal justice systems at federal, state, and local levels. It acts as an advocate for the needs of local criminal justice systems. Its publications include a number of archived reports on a variety of criminal justice topics as well as the periodicals *NCJA InfoLetter, Justice Bulletin, Policy and Practice*, the *Beacon: Newsletter of the Justice Information Sharing Practitioners*, and *InfoSys: Newsletter of the National Association for Justice Information Systems*.

National Criminal Justice Reference Service (NCJRS)
PO Box 6000, Rockville, MD 20849-6000
(800) 851-3420
Web site: www.ncjrs.gov

The National Criminal Justice Reference Service is a reference resource that compiles information dealing with criminal justice issues. Its goal is to support those who are creating policies and programs dealing with criminal justice as well as those who are researching the subject. Its Web site offers a range of services, including a question and answer section, many publications and reports that are available for download, and a database of article abstracts.

Supreme Court of the United States
Public Information Officer
  Washington, DC 20543
(202) 479-3211
Web site: www.supremecourtus.gov

The Supreme Court of the United States is the highest court of appeals in the United States. It hears cases that have made their way through the lower courts and have petitioned the Court for a final appeal. The Court's Web site offers a full description of the workings of the Court as well as a listing of the Court's docket, opinions from recent cases, and information on how to contact or visit the Supreme Court.

U.S. Department of Justice (DOJ)
950 Pennsylvania Ave. NW
  Washington, DC 20530-0001
(202) 514-2000
e-mail: AskDOJ@usdoj.gov
Web site: www.usdoj.gov

The mission of the U.S. Department of Justice is to enforce the law, defend the United States against foreign and domestic threats, and work with local and state governments to fight crime, punish the guilty, and protect the rights of the innocent. Its Web site offers a collection of publications, legal documents, and strategic plans dealing with numerous issues pertaining to criminal justice as well as speeches and testimony from various officials.

For Further Research

Books

Michal R. Belknap, *The Supreme Court Under Earl Warren, 1953–1969*. Columbia: University of South Carolina Press, 2004.

Bureau of National Affairs, *The Criminal Law Revolution and Its Aftermath, 1960–1977*. Washington, DC: Bureau of National Affairs, 1978.

Richard C. Cortner, *The Supreme Court and the Second Bill of Rights: The Fourteenth Amendment and the Nationalization of Civil Liberties*. Madison: University of Wisconsin Press, 1981.

Samuel Dash, *The Intruders: Unreasonable Searches and Seizures from King John to John Ashcroft*. New Brunswick, NJ: Rutgers University Press, 2004.

Rolando V. del Carmen and Jeffery T. Walker, *Briefs of Leading Cases in Law Enforcement*. Cincinnati: Anderson, 1997.

Jim Fisher, *Fall Guys: False Confessions and the Politics of Murder*. Carbondale: Southern Illinois University Press, 1996.

Ron Fridell, *Miranda Law: The Right to Remain Silent*. New York: Marshall Cavendish Benchmark, 2005.

John Galloway, *Criminal Justice and the Burger Court*. New York: Facts On File, 1978.

———, *The Supreme Court and the Rights of the Accused*. New York: Facts On File, 1973.

Susan Dudley Gold, *Miranda v. Arizona (1966): Suspects' Rights*. New York: Twenty-First Century, 1995.

G. Edward Griffin, *The Great Prison Break: The Supreme Court Leads the Way.* Boston: Western Islands, 1968.

John E. Hess, *Interviewing and Interrogation for Law Enforcement.* Cincinnati: Anderson, 1997.

Morton J. Horwitz, *The Warren Court and the Pursuit of Justice: A Critical Issue.* New York: Hill and Wang, 1998.

Peter Irons and Stephanie Guitton, eds., *May It Please the Court: The Most Significant Oral Arguments Made Before the Supreme Court Since 1955.* New York: New Press, 1993.

Jacob W. Landynski, *Search and Seizure and the Supreme Court: A Study in Constitutional Interpretation.* Baltimore: Johns Hopkins Press, 1966.

Richard A. Leo and George C. Thomas III, *The Miranda Debate: Law, Justice, and Policing.* Boston: Northeastern University Press, 1998.

Frederick P. Lewis, *The Context of Judicial Activism: The Endurance of the Warren Court Legacy in a Conservative Age.* Lanham, MD: Rowman & Littlefield, 1999.

Robert M. Maslow, *"Coddling Criminals" Under the Warren Court.* Washington, DC: Coiner, 1969.

Tony Mauro, *Illustrated Great Decisions of the Supreme Court.* Washington, DC: CQ, 2000.

Darien A. McWhirter, *Search, Seizure, and Privacy.* Phoenix: Oryx, 1994.

Michael J. Perry, *We the People: The Fourteenth Amendment and the Supreme Court.* New York: Oxford University Press, 1999.

John Earl Pratt, *Robbery, Rape, Burglary, Riot, Murder, Arson, Bombings; the Earl Warren Supreme Court.* Columbus, OH: Bourke House, 1970.

Harry N. Scheiber, *Earl Warren and the Warren Court: The Legacy in American and Foreign Law*. Berkeley: Institute of Governmental Studies Press, University of California, 2005.

Bernard Schwartz, *The Warren Court: A Retrospective*. New York: Oxford University Press, 1996.

Roger W. Shuy, *The Language of Confession, Interrogation, and Deception*. Thousand Oaks, CA: Sage, 1998.

Christopher E. Smith et al., *The Supreme Court, Crime, and the Ideal of Equal Justice*. New York: P. Lang, 2003.

Gary L. Stuart, *Miranda: The Story of America's Right to Remain Silent*. Tucson: University of Arizona Press, 2004.

Mark V. Tushnet, *The Warren Court in Historical and Political Perspective*. Charlottesville: University Press of Virginia, 1993.

Melvin I. Urofsky, *The Warren Court: Justices, Rulings, and Legacy*. Santa Barbara, CA: ABC-CLIO, 2001.

Web Sites

National Archive of Criminal Justice Data (NACJD) (www.icpsr.umich.edu/NACJD). The NACJD is a database of information related to criminal justice and criminology. It provides searchable data on a variety of topics.

OYEZ Project (www.oyez.org). The OYEZ Project is a multimedia database of Supreme Court cases. It contains case summaries and over two thousand hours of audio recordings of actual cases.

Sourcebook of Criminal Justice Statistics (www.albany.edu/sourcebook). The Sourcebook of Criminal Justice Statistics is a collection of data from over one hundred sources dealing with a variety of criminal justice subjects.

Index

mistaken arguments for, 28–29

compromises on, 43–45

does not hinder Fourth Amendment protection, 40–42

federal-state cooperation on, 24–25

government observance of laws and, 25–26

New York's rejection of, 36–37

political power of law enforcement and, 42–43

protection of privacy and, 23–24

rejection of alternatives to, 37–38

remedy to, erosion of rights and, 45–46

Feldman v. United States (1944), 24

Fifth Amendment, 82
exclusionary rule and, 24–25
privilege against self-incrimination in, 71–72
protections found in, 13, 69–70, 73, 104
are not absolute, 14–15
self-incrimination and, 69–70
voluntary statements are not barred by, 79

Fourteenth Amendment
application of exclusionary rule to states and, 28–30
Due Process Clause of, 21–23, 32
interrogation process and, 82

Fourth Amendment
"consensual encounters" and, 64
Court's discussion of, in *Terry*, 167, 168
covers only tangible items, 122–24

does not protect against all searches and seizures, 147

Due Process Clause of Fourteenth Amendment and, 21, 22

efforts to limit scope of, 134–35

exclusionary rule and, 14, 23, 24–25, 29–30, 32, 40–42, 45

extends to recording of oral statements, 116

impact of *Katz* on, 139–40

Katz's modern approach to, 132–34

limitations on search and seizure in, 154–55

misinterpretation of, in *Katz* decision, 128–29

not applied to state courts, 18–19

property-based literalism approach to, 131–32

property law and, 137–38

protection of people and not places in, 111, 141–42, 149

protection of people and places in, 136–37

protections found in, 13, 114, 115, 149
are not absolute, 14–15

reasonable expectation of privacy and, 111–12, 143–44

"reasonable" search and seizures and, 158, 159

stop and frisks and, 151–53

Fourth Lateran Council (1215), 104

Frankfurter, Felix, 37, 107, 108

Friendly, Fred W., 49

Gideon v. Wainwright (1963), 75

Goldman v. United States (1942), 116, 132, 140